BLOCK 3
'ENGLISHNESS'

Prepared for the course team by Angus Calder, Roger Day and Graham Martin

A319

Arts: a third
level course

The course team

Richard Allen (author)
Jenny Bardwell (BBC producer)
Richard Bessel (author)
Dinah Birch (author)
Angus Calder (author)
Kate Clements (editor)
Tony Coe (BBC series producer and author)
Charles Cooper (BBC producer)
Tony Coulson (Library)
Abigail Croydon (editor)
Roger Day (author)
Andrew Ferguson (course manager)
Margaret Harvey (block rapporteur)
Cicely Palser Havely (author)
Pam Higgins (graphic designer)
Barbara Humphreys (secretary)
G.D. Jayalakshimi (BBC producer)
Denis Johnson (tuition group chair)
Maggie Lawson (Project Control)
Beth Martin (BBC producer)

Graham Martin (course team chair, author)
Mags Noble (BBC producer)
Sue O'Connor (secretary)
W.R. Owens (editor of anthologies)
John Pettit (editor)
Michael Rossington (author)
Betty Talks (BBC producer)
Nora Tomlinson (tuition group)
Dennis Walder (author)
Keith Whitlock (author)
Amanda Willett (BBC producer)
Richard Wilson (block rapporteur)

Consultants

Dr Pamela Morris, member of the Open University's teaching and counselling staff (block assessor)
Professor Michael Wood, department of English literature at the University of Exeter (external assessor)

The Open University
Walton Hall, Milton Keynes MK7 6AA

First published 1991. Reprinted 1995

Copyright © 1991 The Open University

All rights reserved. No part of this publication may be reproduced, stored in a retrieval system or transmitted in any form or by any means, without written permission from the publisher or a licence from the Copyright Licensing Agency Limited. Details of such licences (for reprographic reproduction) may be obtained from the Copyright Licensing Agency Ltd, 33–34 Alfred Place, London WC1E 7DP.

Typeset in 10 on 12 point Palatino.

Printed in the United Kingdom by Page Bros, Norwich

ISBN 0 7492 1037 0

This block is part of an Open University course. The complete list of blocks is given at the end of this binding.

If you have not enrolled on the course and would like to buy this or other Open University material, please write to Open University Educational Enterprises Limited, 12 Cofferidge Close, Stony Stratford, Milton Keynes MK11 1BY, United Kingdom.

If you wish to enquire about enrolling as an Open University student, please write to: The Admissions Office, The Open University, PO Box 48, Walton Hall, Milton Keynes MK7 6AB, United Kingdom

Contents

(Angus Calder wrote Sections 2 and 3; Roger Day wrote Sections 1 and 5–9; Graham Martin wrote Section 4)

    Required reading 5
    Broadcasts/cassettes 5
    Aims and objectives 5

1 What is 'Englishness'? 6
    Englishness, education and gender 11
    The English language and the *Dictionary of National Biography* 14
    National characteristics (or stereotypes) 16
    Conclusion 18

2 Georgian poetry 19
    The social background 23
    Charlotte Mew and Edmund Blunden 25
    Edward Thomas 26

3 P.G. Wodehouse: 'Indian Summer of an Uncle' 32
    Why 'Jeeves'? 32
    Reading Jeeves 32
    Language and discourse 34
    Gender, power and aunts 35
    Jeeves, Wooster, class and Englishness 37

4 W.H. Auden 39
    'England … where nobody is well' 40
    Auden and Modernism 48

5 Consciousness in fiction 55

6 Graham Greene: *England Made Me* 59
    Anthony and Kate 62
    Krogh 71
    The economic background 72
    Greene's prose style in *England Made Me* 74
    Summary 75

7 John Betjeman 76

8   Evelyn Waugh: *Officers and Gentlemen*   85
  Officers *and* gentlemen?   89
  Characters in *Officers and Gentlemen*   90
  Class and the 'people's war'   94
  Gender in *Officers and Gentlemen*   95
  Moral issues in *Officers and Gentlemen*   97
  Humour in *Officers and Gentlemen*   100
  Summary of Book One   104

9   Meaning and interpretation   106

10 References   110
  The Jeeves canon: a note   112

Required reading

Graham Greene (1970a) *England Made Me*, Penguin, first published in 1935 (set book)

Evelyn Waugh (1964) *Officers and Gentlemen*, Penguin, first published in 1955 (set book)

W.H. Auden and John Betjeman, poems (in the Poetry Anthology)

Georgian poems (in the Poetry Anthology)

P.G. Wodehouse, 'Indian Summer of an Uncle' (in the Prose Anthology)

From the A319 Reader
Neville Cardus, 'Good days'
E.M. Forster, 'Notes on the English character'
Asa Briggs, 'The English: how the nation sees itself'
George Orwell, 'The Lion and the Unicorn'
Virginia Woolf, 'Women and nationalism'
W.H. Auden, 'Memorable speech'
E.D. Hirsch, Jr., 'The Babel of interpretations'
Stanley Fish, 'Interpreting the *Variorum*'
Robert Scholes, 'Who cares about the text?'
(The A319 Reader is *Literature in the Modern World*, edited by Dennis Walder, 1990, Oxford University Press/The Open University.)

Broadcasts/cassettes

TV4 *Crossing the Border: images of England in the 1930s* (linked with Sections 1, 2 and 4)

TV5 *Left and Write: recalling the 30s* (linked with Sections 1, 3, 4, 5 and 6)

Radio 4 *Home and Abroad* (linked with Sections 5, 6 and 8)

Radio 5 *Is There a Text in this Programme? Meaning and interpretation* (linked with Section 9)

Audio-cassette 2 Side 1, 'Betjeman and Auden' (linked with Sections 4 and 7)

(See also the Broadcast and Cassette Notes.)

Aims and objectives

This block has three principal aims:

(a) to guide your reading of the set texts – Wodehouse's 'Indian Summer of an Uncle', Greene's *England Made Me*, Waugh's *Officers and Gentlemen*, Georgian poetry, and the poems of Auden and Betjeman;

(b) to analyse versions of the English 'national identity' and to examine texts in which it finds various forms of expression;

(c) to introduce two aspects of the formal study of literature – how a writer conveys the consciousness of his/her characters in fiction, and how we decide that one interpretation is more 'correct' than another.

All the sections interlink: for example, you will need to apply the discussion of 'national characteristics' in Section 1 to your study of Graham Greene's *England Made Me* in Section 6. Your study of how *consciousness* is presented in fiction, and the subtleties of different *interpretations* in Section 9, will be applicable to fiction studied in the rest of the course.

The introduction to 'Meaning and interpretation' in Section 9 is included in this block so that you can concentrate on the issues involved and then take the ideas forward to apply to texts later in the course. Radio 5 *Is There a Text in this Programme? Meaning and interpretation* relates the issues of Section 9 to the texts in this block.

1 What is 'Englishness'?

1.1 This first section of this block investigates the theme of 'Englishness'. After a preliminary discussion, I shall ask you to read a number of items contained in the Reader and these will form the basis of a debate. 'Englishness' is a vast subject which has filled volumes. The various constructions of 'Englishness' are discussed as a preliminary exercise to an examination of versions of it embedded in the texts that follow. A number of these texts are from the 1930s, which is the chronological focus adopted for this block. The reason for choosing the 1930s is that this was the period in which an idea of Englishness inherited from the era of the 1914–18 war came under attack. Edward Thomas had no problem with the notion: Greene and Auden in the aftermath of the First World War did. Similarly, the Second World War called into question a whole scale of values for Waugh, and he expressed this doubt in *Officers and Gentlemen*. (The broadcasting for this block is essential to an understanding of this context.) With limited space, the terms of the debate are narrower than ideally one would wish – there are only two female voices, and none from the working class. There is, you might say, a 'partiality of knowledge' on the subject. What right, you might reasonably ask, has E.M. Forster or Neville Cardus to take it upon himself to 'speak for the nation'? But then you might go further and ask whether anyone has the right to do this, except in times of national crisis. The politician Ken Livingstone made this point on BBC Radio 4 in 1988, when he admitted that he identified Englishness with a small élite who held all political and financial power:

> INTERVIEWER   But what you've done is say they've commandeered the notion of being English.
>
> LIVINGSTONE   Yes, and frankly since they've done that I will seek my satisfactions by embracing the world.

1.2 If, however, the debate is to get under way, you have to start somewhere: the terms chosen here are in relation to education and gender, language and national characteristics. You might have chosen different categories and ended up with a different view of 'Englishness'. This doesn't matter – in fact, it could be a good thing for it should encourage you to continue and develop the debate in terms beyond those discussed in this block. The television programmes should also help to do this for, in TV4 *Crossing the Border*, Angus Calder shows a less 'upper-class' version of Englishness than the Reader items for this block suggest. (Even the left-wing Orwell went to Eton.) As Angus Calder commented on reading an earlier draft of this block:

> Some of the most characteristic expressions of the cult of rural England came from the Labour movement, from Blatchford's Clarion Cycling Clubs through the Ramblers Association (*always* radical left!). Priestley, a *prime*

exponent of rural Englishness, was *not* a public school toff and *was* a man of the left. Cardus was self-educated lower class. I believe that 'Englishness' of the Georgian sort was always repressive and socially reactionary, even when the left took it up. But the left *were* fighting, many of them, to capture it for the 'working class' (for example, besides those I've mentioned, C. Day Lewis, Humphrey Jennings).

ACTIVITY

Now, I suggest that you cast your mind back to Section 4 of Block 1 where Graham Martin explained the place of themes in the course. Briefly, what were the main points he made?

DISCUSSION

'Englishness', Graham Martin explained, is not a concept invented in the twentieth century, and nationalism is not unique to this country. It is in the course, as a theme, he argued, because 'English literature became a major subject for university study at the beginning of the twentieth century'. It started in the Victorian period as early as 1830 when Ruskin studied Spenser and Pope, among others, at King's College, London, and, in the form we know it, became part of the Oxbridge syllabus at the beginning of the twentieth century. Outside universities the reading of English literature was also thought important as a means of promoting national unity. This particular debate (which continues at the time of writing with the introduction of a national curriculum) is one we shall be looking at more closely later. But the idea of Englishness is not a static concept: as Graham Martin pointed out in his final paragraphs, it shifts, its meaning changes within the years covered by this course 'in response to the complex and many-sided historical process stretching between 1920 and 1980. The changeable nature of the concept goes back, of course, far beyond 1920. Writing about the subject for a course the Open University presented in the 1980s (A403 *Arts and Society in Britain since the Thirties*), Angus Calder defined two versions of Englishness: one was the 'radical tradition' of Milton, Bunyan, Blake and Lawrence, 'heterodox in religion, prone to heresy or atheism, addicted to personal liberty, yet also drawn to visions of communal harmony'. The second was the 'newer tradition, a product of the nineteenth century', producing the 'New Englishman' formed by his public school – the 'gentleman', who stood for 'fair play', 'was devoted to team games, indifferent to artistic values, and contemptuous of ideas, especially foreign ideas'.

1.3 The debate goes on. Indeed, it could be said to be part of our national life, a continual process of self-redefinition. The popular programme *Any Questions?* on BBC Radio 4 illustrates one aspect of the debate well: in 1943 the Lord Provost of Edinburgh could be heard talking about the 'good taste' of the 'masses', as shown in the ordinary Englishman's liking for cricket and his garden, thereby making them into national icons. Forty or so years later, the same class issue (implicit in any reference to 'the masses') was still being hotly debated in another BBC radio programme, *Start the Week,* by the deputy leader of the Labour Party and assorted guests. The search goes on in books, essays, articles in academic magazines, features in popular papers, television programmes (including TV4 *Crossing the Border*), all attempting to pin down the 'national characteristic'.

1.4 Having studied much of this material, it now seems to me that what is most missing from all these attempts is a sufficiently clear sense of method and an understanding (or an admission, perhaps) of motivation: there is

BLOCK 3 'ENGLISHNESS'

insufficient self-awareness and a lack of explicitness as to *what* is being looked for and *why*. Another way of putting this is to state that any definition of 'Englishness' is, whether seen as such or not, at heart an ideological statement. Ideology is the theme of Block 4, but it is not an undue trespass on that territory to attempt a preliminary definition of the subject for the working purposes of this block.

1.5 Graham Martin introduced the subject in Section 8 of Block 2, where he discussed the problem of the 'ideological' in 'literary' texts. For the purposes of Block 3, I shall be using the word 'ideology' to mean any *set of beliefs* about religion, science, and behaviour, without reference as to whether or not they are 'true'. To quote from another Open University course (DE354 *Beliefs and Ideologies*, Study Guide 2, p.7): 'An ideology is any beliefs, understanding, definitions, explanations which form a set, and which are used to explain, interpret or produce an understanding of how things work in the social world, and which inform social practice.' But, the author goes on to warn, this does not mean '*any* set of beliefs' for 'Ideology cannot be neutral since knowledge always entails power, and the partiality of knowledge is one of the main sources of the power of ideology'.

1.6 Let me illustrate this definition of ideology by asking you to consider an extract from *The Heart of England* by Edward Thomas, the Welsh poet whose work Angus Calder considers in Section 2. Does his nationality have any bearing on his perception of England?

> How nobly the ploughman and the plough and three horses, two chestnuts and a white leader, glide over the broad swelling field in the early morning! Under the dewy, dark-green woodside they wheel, pause and go out into the strong light again, and they seem one and glorious, as if the all breeding earth had just sent them up out of her womb, mighty, splendid and something grim, with darkness and primitive forces clinging about them, and the dark in the horses' manes...
>
> Richard the ploughman is worthy of his plough and team ... But Richard is no ordinary man, for he is happy and proud ... And ah! to see him and his team all dark and large and heroic against the sky ... is to see one who is in league with sun and wind and rain to make odours fume richly from the ancient altar, to keep earth going in beauty and fruitfulness for still more years.
>
> (Thomas, 1906, pp.21–5)

ACTIVITY

I should explain that *The Heart of England* is illustrated (by H.L. Richardson) with many misty coloured plates of country cottages, lanes, horses, and so on. Which *key words* can you pick out and what *set of beliefs* underlies these passages?

DISCUSSION

The *key words* I would pick out are: nobly, glorious, breeding earth, primitive forces, worthy, happy, proud, ancient, altar.

Taken together they constitute a strong (if vague) statement, suggesting that England is some kind of new Eden in harmony with deep mysterious forces, and that this is an excellent state of affairs. This particular kind of pastoralism (that is, a belief that all things are, or should be, centred on 'nature' and the countryside) is the ideology behind such writing. It is a belief that was discussed in TV2 and one that you will be meeting in various forms over and over again.

1 WHAT IS 'ENGLISHNESS'?

1.7 Thomas's picture of England in 1906 is a curious blend of myth, nostalgia and fantasy centred on an unabashed pastoralism. What he describes is an idyll in which everyone lives in tune with 'nature'. The only *town* that is mentioned at the start of the book is 'Town', that is, London, and then only as somewhere to be left behind in the search for true national identity.

1.8 To help you see this account for what it is, an example of the 'partiality of knowledge' referred to above, let me remind you that other things were happening in the England of 1906 – a general election, for instance, which saw the return of a huge Liberal majority to the House of Commons and the start of legislation which would eventually bring old age pensions through a national insurance scheme. It was also the year that saw the first Labour MPs and the emergence of the women's suffrage movement in Britain, though you would never suspect anything of the kind from this account of the country. In fact, the 'heart' of England was very far from the countryside, and Thomas's version, if it ever existed, was about 200 years before the time of writing. His book is an expression of a full-blown national myth which he liked to think of as his England.

1.9 Twenty years on the same myth was being perpetuated. In his book, *In Search of England* (1927), again illustrated by pictures of country lanes and cart-horses, H.V. Morton argued that to survive in 'the modern/industrial world' the country needed as well 'a contented and flourishing *peasantry*' (my italics). He went on to illustrate what he meant in a chapter on 'how wireless comes to Arcady'. (Note the place name: 'Arcadia' was a district in southern Greece, and the term came to stand for an ideal, rustic setting.)

> 'This wireless has made a rare difference to us,' said the farmer as he sat in his muddy boots and leggings, turning knobs and switching valves off and on…
>
> 'He's a beauty, he is!' said the old man pointing with his pipe stem to the valve set. 'Durin' that bit of a strike you had up in Lonnun we could hear 'xactly all that wor passing as clear as I can see you, sor.'

1.10 This anecdote is more than just a piece of humour, though it is that – if in a way other than Morton intended. It is also highly political: not only does Morton patronize the farmer (a peasant can operate modern technology), he also reduces the General Strike of 1926 to 'that bit of a strike', minimizing it as insignificant. The ideological slant of Morton's writing is not simply pastoral; it is also positively anti-urban. Towns are where strikes take place, and where people come from who behave on village greens with a 'barbaric lack of manners'.

1.11 As a contrast, please read the following passage.

> Britain, the most conservative major society in Europe, had a culture in its own image: mediocre and inert. The ataraxy [stoical indifference] of this culture is manifest in any international context. But it is a culture of which the Left in Britain had largely been a passive spectator, and at times a deluded accomplice. Twentieth-century British culture was by and large made against it. Yet the Left has never truly questioned this 'national' inheritance which is one of the most enduring bonds of its subordination. But this duty remains on the Agenda of any serious socialist movement in Britain that may emerge from the debris of the past.
>
> (Anderson, 1969, p.4)

ACTIVITY

In this openly political comment, what 'ideology' would you say emerges, and which are the *key words*?

BLOCK 3 'ENGLISHNESS'

DISCUSSION

In a very simple sense, the descriptive word 'conservative' in this passage equals 'bad', 'Left' equals failed aspirations while 'serious socialist' equals 'good', and Britain is seen, in relation to other nations, as moribund. The key words are conservative, mediocre, serious socialist, debris; and the ideology behind the writing is, in a broad sense, socialism. Using the word 'culture' in a general way, Anderson has constructed a version of English history to illustrate his political point of view in the same way that Thomas and Morton constructed versions of England to support their forms of pastoralism. You will remember from TV2 *English, whose English?* how Graham Martin examined 'constructed images'. What was done there in terms of images we can see being done here in words: in each case, a deliberately limited account is given which omits the positive qualities (Anderson) or the negative ones (Thomas).

1.12 We shall pursue this investigation of constructions of 'Englishness' by means of extracts printed in the Reader. The discussion will focus on the following: education and gender, language and the *Dictionary of National Biography*, and national characteristics. The point of this exercise is to relate discoveries made about 'Englishness' to the appearance of the theme in the *texts* that follow. For example, when you come to read *England Made Me* in Section 6 of this block, you will be able to use the conclusions you have come to about 'national characteristics', just as you will be able to take your knowledge of Edward Thomas to Angus Calder's study of his poetry in the next section.

1.13 You may have noticed that so far the quotations have been using the words 'British' and 'English' interchangeably, yet this is hardly fair to the inhabitants of Scotland, Wales and Northern Ireland. The theme we are studying in Block 3 is *'Englishness'*, the qualities ascribed to English people and their myths in versions constructed in the discourse of the time, in the counties within the borders of England, in the period covered by this course. This is a deliberately narrow focus, for to try to do more would be confusing and would trespass on areas to be covered by other blocks, such as Block 5 *End of Empire* and Block 6 *New Writings in English*, where the English language of the set texts is used by writers of other nations. Remember, too, that Englishness is a concept that can change with time (as Graham Martin pointed out), and that how you see it depends to a large extent on where you stand: the outsider's view of the English is not always their own, as this extract from Doris Lessing's *In Pursuit of the English* illustrates:

> I came into contact with the English very early in life, because as it turns out, my father was an Englishman. I put it like this, instead of making a claim or deprecating a fact, because it was not until I had been in England for some time I understood my father.
>
> I wouldn't like to say that I brooded over his character; that would be putting it strongly, but I certainly spent a good part of my childhood coming to terms with it. I must confess ... that I concluded at the age of about six my father was mad...
>
> I decided my father was mad on such evidence as that, at various times and for varying periods he believed that (a) One should only drink water that had stood long enough in the direct sun to collect its invisible magic rays (b) One should only sleep in a bed in such a position that those health-giving electric currents which continuously dart back and forth from Pole to Pole can pass directly through one's body, instead of losing their strength by being forced off course...

As I said, it was only some time after I reached England, I understood that
this – or what I had taken to be – splendidly pathological character would
merge into the local scene without so much as a surprised snarl from
anyone.

(Lessing, 1968, pp.7–8)

1.14   The particular qualities that Doris Lessing seems to be isolating here are
the eccentricity of the English character, and also tolerance – people are
allowed to hold cranky views. The idea of nationality has a fairly recent
history, as Graham Martin explained in his introduction to the theme in
Block 1.

Englishness, education and gender

1.15   Character and identity, whether individual or of a nation, are to a great
extent formed through *education*, the first of my four categories, and so I want
to spend some time looking at how and why *nationalism* has figured in
curricula over the period covered by the course.

1.16   In his book, *The Social Mission of English Criticism 1848–1932* (1983), the
critic and cultural historian Chris Baldick explains how the First World War
produced a sense of English nationalism in which English literature was
allowed to play a central part, and that consequently the study of English
literature assumed a new importance. Associated with this was a wave of
anti-German sentiment which resulted in a rejection of German academic
interests, among which was philology. More positively, this movement
produced a pride in the English language. At the same time, English studies
were becoming 'professionalized' by academics such as Ernest de Selincourt,
who saw in literature, and especially in poetry, a means of spiritual support
in times of national crisis, a way of creating national unity.

1.17   Then, after the Great War, came the Newbolt Report (1921). This was
the report of a government committee chaired by the poet Henry Newbolt,
which had been set up to investigate the teaching of English in schools
(similar to the Kingman Report of 1988 which we shall come to presently).
This report was widely read and discussed both within and without the world
of education. While recognizing the contempt often displayed by the ignorant
for what they perceived as literature, the authors nevertheless saw it as a
means of promoting social unity. Taking this even further, the report took the
view (mentioned by Graham Martin in TV2) that university teachers of the
subject had a mission to the population as a whole, since 'literature is not just
a subject for academic study but one of the chief temples of the human spirit,
in which all should worship'. Needless to say, pretensions of this kind did not
go unchallenged!

1.18   Nevertheless, it was from the 1920s onwards that English literature
became established as a subject for university study, as Brian Doyle explains
in an essay called 'The hidden history of English studies':

> As part of these processes of specialisation and professionalisation the status
> of the 'text' became increasingly important, and from the 1920s onwards
> was enshrined as the central and supposedly objective element in the study
> of literature within higher education, supported by the equally objective-
> looking notion of 'literary value'. At this moment, and from this perspective
> only, English literature as a discipline in higher education shook off much of
> what had previously been its role (as one aspect of the study of the
> 'national character') and emerged as an autonomous academic discipline
> almost exclusively concerned with the study of its own texts.
>
> (in Widdowson, 1982, pp.27–8)

1 WHAT IS
'ENGLISHNESS'?

BLOCK 3 'ENGLISHNESS'

1.19 It was in 1917 that 'at Cambridge members of Senate met to debate the formation of an English Tripos' (Mulhern, 1979, pp.3–4). Brian Doyle has explained in 'The invention of English' how English became an 'autonomous academic discipline'.

> In 1880 English as an autonomous academic discipline did not exist. Although since the 1820s a chair of English Language and Literature had been established at University College, London, and a handful of similar chairs (usually under the title of 'English and History' had been added during the intervening decades, such innovations both in their characteristic methods and subject matter reached back to an older tradition of teaching 'Rhetoric' with an added emphasis from the middle of the century on historical and philological studies. The period of real growth and transformation took place after 1880 and coincided with the development of the new 'provincial' college sector outside the ancient universities of Oxford and Cambridge, which set in motion the rise of a number of new departments of 'modern' knowledge. However, by 1920, English in a substantially adapted form when compared with 'English Language and Literature' or 'English and History' had come to be seen by public administrators, politicians, academics and 'men-of-letters' not only as a necessary constituent of a modern national system of education, but even in many cases as its most essential core element.
>
> (in Colls and Dodd, 1986, p.92)

1.20 In the same chapter, Doyle explains how English eventually overtook Classics as a major discipline:

> From the 1840s the inferior position of English language and literature began to be questioned, mostly by scholars working outside the ancient universities of England, but it was only during the early decades of the present century that English Studies (or, more simply, 'English') in its recognisably modern disciplinary form began to offer an educationally significant challenge to the intellectual and cultural prestige long invested in classics.
>
> (p.92)

1.21 The point that emerges from the accounts of Baldick and Doyle of the years during and after the First World War is that while the study of English at school level continued to be seen as useful for unifying the nation, in universities the subject had shaken off this role and established itself as a discipline concentrating on texts. But if the universities, in the end, got from 'Englishness' to 'English', the schools, particularly the so-named public schools for boys (that is, private boarding schools), were very much concerned with a sense of national identity.

ACTIVITY

Please now read 'Notes on the English character' (1920) by E.M. Forster in the Reader (pp.176–7). Sum up in a sentence or two the point Forster is making about the national character. What objections might be made to it?

DISCUSSION

Forster's view is that 'Englishness' is essentially middle class and that the middle classes (though he really means ruling classes) are epitomized by the public-school system which produced men with 'undeveloped hearts'. The possible objection I had in mind is a very simple one: Forster has simply appropriated the term for his own purposes and argument. His is a 'middle-class' version of Englishness and cannot really claim to be the 'essential' version.

1.22   Nevertheless, Forster was not alone in this view as this extract from an essay by Philip Dodd, 'Englishness and the national culture', shows:

> First, a brief sketch of the dominant English. The centrality of educational institutions for the control and dissemination of a national identity hardly needs stressing ... In 1929, Bernard Darwin, in one of a large number of books around that time about the public school system, said that, whatever one's views of it, 'it is really to a great extent the English character we are criticising'.
>
> (in Colls and Dodd, 1986, p.3)

1.23   A similar objection might be made to the Darwinian view of the 'English character': it is being related solely to the 'higher' classes, regardless of the fact that numerically the working class forms by far the larger part of the population, half of whom at least are women. But, as Dodd goes on to argue, the public-school system in alliance with the universities of Oxford and Cambridge (where pupils were eventually sent for higher education)

> did not, of course, select only in terms of class but also – like Oxford and Cambridge – in terms of gender. (The cornerstone of the curriculum, classics, was seen as unsuitable for women.) A great deal has usefully been written about the public school system, but what is important in this argument is its construction of masculinity, and its exclusion of women – within the terms of the argument, the exclusion of certain qualities which had been ceded to the female. Indeed, one might go so far as to argue that the core of the curriculum *was* masculinity.
>
> (p.5)

1.24   In this way, 'Englishness' becomes a male possession, and one associated with activity rather than intellectual pursuits:

> In 1872, W. Turley in the journal *The Dark Blue* urged support for masculinity, relating nationhood, gender and appropriate activity in his argument that 'a nation of effeminate, enfeebled bookworms, scarcely forms the most effective bulwark of a nation's liberties'. 'Vigorous, manly and English' was the popular collocation.
>
> (pp.5–6)

1.25   Turley's attitude was to persist beyond his time of writing. This preoccupation even extended to literary style:

> Given that males had at least to read and write (but not too much), they must cultivate a 'masculine' style, as many of the books on style made clear. For instance, Arthur Quiller Couch could say in one of the series of lectures at the University of Cambridge: 'Generally use transitive verbs, that strike their objects and use them in the active voice ... For as a rough law, by his use of the straight verb and by economy of adjectives, you can tell a man's style, if it be masculine or neuter, writing or composition.'
>
> (p.6)

1.26   So, to sum up, to be English in the public-school sense is to be male, not working class, and to express that maleness through style. Then, as the grammar schools were modelled on the public schools, the effect of this idea of Englishness on the national culture became widespread.

1.27   But this male, comfortably placed version of national identity did not go unchallenged. Inevitably it made femininity seem peripheral, nonproductive, indeed hardly a state at all. Virginia Woolf, living in Bloomsbury in the years after the Great War in which so many men had perished, was moved to reflect on the privileged position of the British male. (You will remember that in Block 2, Dinah Birch discussed the novel *Mrs Dalloway* in terms of language and gender.) This is what Virginia Woolf wrote in her collection of essays called *Three Guineas*:

> ...both the Army and the Navy are closed to our sex. We are not allowed to fight. Nor again are we allowed to be members of the Stock Exchange. Thus we can use neither the pressure of force nor the pressure of money. The less direct but still effective weapons which our brothers, as educated men, possess in the diplomatic service, in the Church, are also denied to us. We cannot preach sermons or negotiate treaties ... Not only are we incomparably weaker than the men of our own class; we are weaker than the women of the working class. If the working women of the country were to say: 'If you go to war, we will refuse to make munitions or to help in the production of goods,' the difficulty of war-making would be seriously increased. But if all the daughters of educated men were to down tools tomorrow, nothing essential to the life or to the war-making of the community would be embarrassed.
>
> (Woolf, 1938, pp.23–4)

ACTIVITY

Please now read the short extract from a later part of *Three Guineas* reproduced in the Reader ('Women and nationalism', pp.196–200). How has the position of women influenced Virginia Woolf's feeling about nationality?

DISCUSSION

Quite radically, I would say, to the point where she suggests that only a vestigial sense of being English should, if her ideas were taken literally, remain in women. For, if women are to form an 'Outsiders' Society' without the male appurtenances of committees and meetings, and to adopt an attitude of 'indifference' which in effect would mean pacifism, and if they were to look at how much of England belonged to them, then the daughter of an educated man would have to come to the conclusion that:

> her sex and class has very little to thank England for in the past; not much to thank England for in the present; while the security of her person in the future is highly dubious.
>
> (Reader, p.198)

In the light of these facts, any 'love of England' that remains becomes 'pure, if irrational, emotion'. Virginia Woolf's point is simple but striking: the English institutions are exclusive and male centred. To what extent, you might go on to ask, is that also true of the way Englishness is represented in this block with only two female voices? There is, however, another woman's voice later in the course which could also claim to speak for the theme: your work on Stevie Smith's poetry in Block 7 will form a further contribution to the debate.

The English language and the *Dictionary of National Biography*

1.28 Style, and the use of the English language in general, has long been a preoccupation of those minded to guard and preserve it. You have only to look at the number of organizations that exist for the purpose to see that this is so. There is, for example, the English Association, which was very influential in the Newbolt Report. It was

> ...founded in 1906 by a group of English teachers and scholars ... The Association aims to promote that knowledge and appreciation of English

language and literature, by creating opportunities of co-operation between all those interested in English; by holding lectures, conferences and other meetings; by publishing a journal, books and leaflets; and by forming local branches at home and overseas.

1.29   At the time of writing, 600 individuals and 245 organizations in the United Kingdom belong to the English Association (there is also an overseas membership). In addition, there are other watchdogs of a similar kind.

ACTIVITY

Inherent in the formation of numerous reports and, indeed, of the English Association, is the assumption that the English language *matters*, and needs protecting. A number of public figures think that it does. Why should this be so?

DISCUSSION

One reason would be to save what is an inherited medium of beauty from becoming what Prince Charles has called 'a dismal wasteland of banality, cliché and casual obscenity'. Another has to be that possession of language constitutes power and can be made a means of control. Advertisers in the popular press realize this: take these words from an advertisement for a course called 'Good English – the Language of Success': 'Indeed thousands of talented, intelligent people are held back at work and socially because their command of English does not equal their other abilities ... You will discover how you can dominate each situation.' Notice how the key word here is 'dominate' – again the language of power and control.

For different reasons, the authors of the Newbolt Report also recognized it when they wrote:

> English ... is needed in every Faculty. It is the one subject which for an Englishman has the claim of universality. Without it he cannot attain to full powers either of learning or teaching ... English is not merely an indispensable handmaid without whose assistance neither philosopher, nor chemist, nor classical scholar can do his work properly. It is one of the greatest subjects to which a University can call its students.

Every other subject is mediated through language, including nationhood, which has the closest possible relationship to how words, the primary means of communication, are used.

1.30   The importance of guarding the language is reflected in the setting up of reports on reading (the latest being the Kingman in 1988), and societies to keep the language 'pure'. The business of recording the way language is used resulted in the *New English Dictionary* (1884), which we know as the *Oxford English Dictionary* (1928).

1.31   Another 'national' publication contributing to the nation's sense of itself was the *Dictionary of National Biography* (1885–1900), the work of Sir Leslie Stephen, father of Virginia Woolf. Like the teaching of the use of English, it was weighted towards males. So, yet again, 'Englishness' is not only male but also Establishment, for in both projects 'there was an over-attachment to politicians, civil servants and the military and a neglect of the business-world'

(Doyle, 1986, p.19). Doyle's argument, and he makes it convincingly, is that in the period 1880–1920 (immediately preceding the point where this course begins) 'Englishness was appropriated by and became the responsibility of certain narrowly defined groups and their institutions' (p.21). In this way, a version of 'Englishness', constructed like the other examples considered earlier and all others you may encounter, was current in the early decades of this century. Furthermore, it did not remain confined to the shores of Great Britain since, once English had been established as an autonomous discipline, as Doyle described earlier, it could be exported to educate people in the colonies. Texts and the values they carried could thus be transmitted to other cultures.

National characteristics (or stereotypes)

1.32 Is there such a person as the 'typical' Englishman, Frenchman, German, and so on? Tellers of jokes like to think that there is. 'There was an Englishman, a Scot and a Welshman...', many a comedian has begun. If there is a typical English person, what characterizes him or her? List the qualities you think might be associated with being English, and then see if their opposites might also apply!

ACTIVITY

Please now read the two short pieces by Neville Cardus from 'Good days' in the Reader (pp.171–5). What can you find in them of relevance to the theme of this block, and how do you react to the tone of Cardus's writing, especially in the second piece?

DISCUSSION

Cardus writes in great style with what is obviously a deep love of the game of cricket, and in doing so he evokes a picture of a 'typically English' summer day of the kind you see in TV4 *Crossing the Border*. So far so good, but what struck me most about both pieces was the strong sense of class hierarchy in the intensely male world of cricket: as it developed as a game, those taking part became divided into two classes, the 'Gentlemen', who were amateurs, and the 'Players', who were professionals. Segregation was completed by giving each separate dressing rooms. The gentlemen were likely to have come from public schools – Spooner is 'fresh from Marlborough', and Cardus himself was employed for a while at Shrewsbury School. The old player in 'Batsmanship of Manners' talks in a pronounced dialect, as does William in 'Good Days'. (When you come to study *England Made Me* you will find it useful to refer back to these pieces: Greene paints a rather different picture of the effects of a public-school education.)

1.33 'Good Days' is a more nostalgic piece in which Cardus recalls 'Old William', one of the old school of professional cricketers. Again, class distinctions permeate virtually every detail of the account: William stays in lodgings; he wears heavy, long-lasting boots; he finds writing laborious and reveres the education he himself lacks. In other words he is 'working class' and, inevitably, there is an implicit comparison with Cardus himself, the narrator of the events he recalls, and the result is that it sounds patronizing. The class issue is very relevant to the work you will be doing on John Betjeman's poetry, and the whole concept of the 'gentleman' is at the heart of Waugh's novel *Officers and Gentlemen*, to be considered in Section 8 of this block. These will be useful pieces to refer back to.

ACTIVITY

As George Orwell (born Eric Blair) points out in *England Your England*, 'national characteristics are not easy to pin down'. Please now read the extract from his essay, 'The Lion and the Unicorn', in the Reader (pp.180–89), making a list of the points Orwell makes. Do you take issue with his account at any point, remembering that this version of Englishness was constructed during wartime in 1941?

DISCUSSION

Among his generalizations Orwell notes philistinism, empiricism and tolerance as characteristics, though he later qualifies his point about artistic ability with a note on English literature. The paragraph that pulled me up short was the one that begins, 'But in all societies the common people must live to some extent *against* the existing order'.

ACTIVITY

What assumptions lie behind the idea in this paragraph, and do they have a familiar ring?

DISCUSSION

The phrase 'the common people' assumes that there are at least two sorts of people in England, the exceptional and the ordinary. The 'exceptional' are allied with 'the authorities' and constitute the 'surface'; the ordinary, in turn, are linked with the 'genuinely popular culture' which has an unofficial existence at variance with authority. This, then, is another version of 'establishment Englishness' and its dissidents who, ironically, form the majority. Such an assumption is a variant of that giving rise to the two definitions mentioned at the beginning of this section. Acknowledging what he later calls 'the subtle network of compromises', Orwell then looks to a common factor: respect for 'constitutionalism and legality'. You can follow for yourself his finer distinctions.

ACTIVITY

Did you notice how cross-references can be made from Orwell's essay to TV5 *Left and Write: recalling the 30s*?

DISCUSSION

Orwell's reference to the Spanish Civil War (which had ended only two years before he was writing) sheds an interesting new light on British involvement. In the television programme, the point was made that although it was the poets who got publicity, most of the volunteers were working class. Orwell, who had been one of the combatants in the International Brigade, is pointing out that they received very little moral support from their fellow workers at home. The same indifference, and 'absence in nearly all Englishmen' of 'an ordered system of thought' was responsible, he implies, for the election of the National Government. (You can see clips of the reporting of this election in TV5 *Left and Write*.)

**BLOCK 3
'ENGLISHNESS'**

ACTIVITY

How does Orwell's view that 'its natural leaders were mediocrities' compare with the way they are presented in the clips of film at the time?

DISCUSSION

Orwell is clearly of Julian Symons's opinion and shared his contempt for the National Government, but you could be forgiven for thinking from the film commentary that the 1935 General Election had been a resounding triumph for the country. It is an interesting example of what Orwell describes as 'the governing-class control over the press, the radio and education'.

1.34 Let us now examine another account of Englishness, one that might loosely be described as 'liberal' in the political spectrum.

ACTIVITY

Please now read the edited extract from Asa Brigg's 'The English: how the nation sees itself' (Reader, pp.189–96). As you do so, jot down any relevant thoughts that come to you. Are there, for example, any *particular* qualities to do with 'Englishness' that strike you?

DISCUSSION

Briggs, a social historian, approaches his task in an ordered way, establishing different means of investigating the subject. In his third paragraph he illustrates one method, analysing how other nationalities see the nation by quoting the observations of the American novelist, Henry James, on the 'tone of things' in England. He then points out that England is predominantly a Protestant nation, demanding the right to express dissenting views in various ways. Is this insistence on the right to 'freedom' an English prerogative?

Briggs recognizes the problems inherent in generalizing about national character before proceeding to make valuable points about how 'historians of different political persuasions' have contributed to versions of Englishness with varying degrees of approval or disapproval over the events they interpret. The important point to grasp is that, again, we have constructed versions of the subject which change, not simply with point of view, but also with the passing of time.

Finally, Briggs comes to that pervasive issue in any study of Englishness – the class system. His final paragraph, emphasizing the diversity of English life, illustrates again the stress on freedom to be what you wish, which echoes Doris Lessing's recognition of the tolerance of eccentricity.

Conclusion

1.35 The purpose of this opening section has been to set up the theme of Englishness by discussing various essays and ideas before going on to read poetry and fiction which have been selected as particularly suitable for further exploration of the theme. So, in the next section of the block, Angus Calder discusses Georgian poetry, some of it written by Edward Thomas, whose 'pastoral' view of England you met at the beginning of this section. Then, in his discussion of P.G. Wodehouse's story 'Indian Summer of an Uncle', Angus Calder examines how an author from an English public-school background presents a version of English society to an American audience. In fact, most of the authors of the set texts to be studied in this block had a public-school education and, in the light of this, E.M. Forster's 'Notes on the English character' assumes a particular importance: his version or construction of Englishness centres on the influence of school on the British male (the national character, again, doesn't seem to take account of women). When you come to the novels by Greene and Waugh, you should ask yourself how the legacy of a public-school education makes itself apparent: as you will see, Greene no more approves of it than Forster, but his reasons are different. On another tack, you might ask yourself what influence it had on Auden: can his homosexuality, his rejection of conventional society, and the effect of these on his poetry, be traced to his education? (In TV5 *Left and Write: recalling the 30s*, Julian Symons saw the influence of schooling as highly important in producing a 'select group' of men who became well-known writers.) But keep in mind, too, Angus Calder's reservations about this 'upper-class' version of Englishness and, as you work your way through the rest of the block, consider TV2 *English, whose English?* and TV4 *Crossing the Border*, in which Graham Martin and Angus Calder examine other images of Englishness. The chronological focus of this block is the decade of the thirties, but you could profitably come back to the theme later in the course when you are studying Block 5 *End of Empire*. What did loss of power and a colonial empire do to the idea of Englishness? Where does it stand today? At the beginning of this section, I suggested that you examine your own perspective on this theme. What did you come up with? Try to establish a few clear points of your own before going on to Section 2.

2 *Georgian poetry*

2.1 In Section 1 Roger Day argues that 'Englishness' is a *construction*, often based on an ideological position. 'Georgianism' is a good place to start investigating examples of the construction of 'England' in 'literature', and would-be 'literature'. Its heyday – *c*.1912–30 – coincides with the First World War and its aftermath, and with the beginning of the timespan covered in this course. But its influence persisted strongly for at least half a century, and could be said to have revived recently in that Edward Thomas, a poet with Georgian attributes, is the centre of much critical controversy, with some admirers elevating him above T.S. Eliot as a major figure in twentieth-century verse.

2.2 You may well have come across Georgianism through reading Georgian poems in school anthologies. Sir Algernon Methuen's 1921 *Anthology of Modern Verse*, largely Georgian, was reprinted seventy-eight times in twenty-five years, and was still in print in the 1960s.

2.3 'Georgianism' is a less slippery term than 'Modernism' or 'Romanticism'.

BLOCK 3 'ENGLISHNESS'

Both these latter terms refer to one period in particular (c.1785 to 1830 for 'British Romanticism'), but also suggest an outlook not confined to that period (so that, as Graham Martin has pointed out, a young writer today might think of himself as 'Modernist'). 'Georgian' refers quite simply to 'a new style popular and influential during the reign of King George V, 1910–36'. Its currency as a term began with the first Georgian anthology of verse, edited by Edward Marsh in 1912. Since George V's reign had only just begun, Marsh's choice of title signified 'innovation'. As C.K. Stead points out (1967, p.58), it is important to realize that in 1912 'many of the younger Georgian poets were considered dangerous literary revolutionaries'. Marsh picked, in this and subsequent Georgian anthologies (the last came out in 1922, and altogether forty writers were included), such young talents as Rupert Brooke, who 'committed', as Stead puts it, 'an act of literary vandalism when he wrote about seasickness'. Marsh also published John Masefield, who used 'low' language, D.H. Lawrence, who wrote free verse with sexual content, and Isaac Rosenberg, whose free verse from the trenches expressed deep cynicism about the war. Young Wilfred Owen (1893–1918) was never anthologized by Marsh. But he admired poets who were and wrote exultantly to his mother in December 1917: 'I am held peer by the Georgians, I am held a poet's poet' (Owen, 1967, p.521).

2.4   The Georgians had a most respectable literary genealogy. Besides paying tribute to the still-living Hardy, their work had strong roots in the Romantics, especially Wordsworth, and Victorians, including Matthew Arnold and R.L. Stevenson. We are bound to see some affinity with A.E. Housman (1859–1936), author of *The Shropshire Lad*, and some of the verse on English themes produced by Rudyard Kipling (1865–1936) anticipates Georgianism unmistakably. But in 1912, the Georgians looked like rebels because they challenged the reigning school of imperialistic, patriotic versifiers – Kipling in another vein, Alfred Noyes, Henry Newbolt (responsible for the Newbolt Report discussed in Section 1). They tried to express everyday experience and to look at the world freshly. Politically, they tended to be Liberal. Wilfred Owen, as Stead suggests, was typical of them in his 'attempt to come to terms with immediate experience, sensuous or imaginative, in a language close to common speech' (1967, p.89).

2.5   Their 'revolt' appealed to the general public for generations. But from the 1920s onward its value was savagely denied by critics impressed with what we now call Modernism, and by young intellectuals. Attacked by literary conservatives in the second decade of the century, they were criticized in the third as unadventurous in theme and style. This has remained a standard charge against 'Georgianism' – too *easy*, too 'pleasant'. The charge hardly sticks to Owen's war poetry. But most Georgians weren't as gifted or as honest as Owen.

2.6   Our object in discussing these poems is not only to define 'literary' qualities (or lack of them). It is to consider how writers of this influential tendency constructed an 'England'. The fact that their vision of 'England' had such influence makes them of key significance in regard to 'Englishness' in our century.

ACTIVITY

Please now consider 'All That's Past', a famous poem by Walter de la Mare (1873–1956), a poet commonly associated with the Georgians. Why do you think this was picked as the very first poem in *Poems of Today*, another long lived and widely read anthology, published for the English Association by Sidgwick and Jackson in 1915? What bearing does it have on 'England'? ('Amaranth', incidentally, is a Greek word denoting an immortal flower which never fades.)

All That's Past

Very old are the woods;
   And the buds that break
Out of the brier's boughs,
   When March winds wake,
So old with their beauty are –
   Oh, no man knows
Through what wild centuries
   Roves back the rose.

Very old are the brooks;
   And the rills that rise
Where snow sleeps cold beneath
   The azure skies
Sing such a history
   Of come and gone,
Their every drop is as wise
   As Solomon.

Very old are we men;
   Our dreams are tales
Told in dim Eden
   By Eve's nightingales;
We wake and whisper a while,
   But, the day gone by,
Silence and sleep like fields
   Of amaranth lie.

DISCUSSION

The two questions I put to you probably need to be answered together. The poem might strike an editor of an anthology as particularly significant at the height of the Great War because it combines 'universal' subject matter with the specifically 'English', and therefore patriotic, associations of the 'rose'. Nature is old. The rose is so old that 'no man knows' how far back it 'roves'. (Note that 'rambler' roses are a familiar English flower, and that 'roving' by gypsies and tramps appealed to the Georgians, who tended to be keen 'ramblers'.) England is old. England (in the second stanza) is, therefore, immanently wise, because old nature is wise. England, we may infer, will endure when all of 'we men' alive in England today, have passed over (like so many young men in France) to 'silence and sleep'. By conveying a wider geographical context, certain words – 'Solomon', 'amaranth' – arguably serve to 'universalize' England: English landscape, English wisdom, English 'Eden', English nightingales, English rose. I am not suggesting that this pre-war poem was in any way meant to be propagandist; just that its imagery serves to construct a beautiful notion of wise England such as a people at war might find consolatory.

ACTIVITY

Please now read, in the Poetry Anthology, John Drinkwater's 'Of Greatham'. This was explicitly occasioned by the war, though its selection for Methuen's anthology ensured a long after-life. Drinkwater (1882–1937) had been one of those present at a luncheon party given by Marsh where the idea of Georgian poetry originated. What does this poem convey about 'England' and 'Englishness'?

BLOCK 3
'ENGLISHNESS'

DISCUSSION

The war has somehow invaded the Sussex landscape. The poet has gone there seeking peace. He has found, literally, 'pastoral' peace among grazing 'flocks'. ('Pastor', of course, means 'shepherd'.) Dawn brings 'unbroken peace' when 'from shire to shire' the 'golden song' of birds is heard. But, in the last three stanzas, this 'peace' is presented as transient, lost, past. Thought of the war ('nations marketing in death') transforms the 'very wind' to sounds of mourning. Only the end of war can restore that peace among Sussex 'roses'.

'Englishness' here centres on a southern 'shire'. This is characteristic of Georgianism, or most of it. The rural counties from Kent across to Devon, north to Shropshire, across to East Anglia, are the English heartland. Hilaire Belloc's remark in a popular poem that the industrial Midlands are 'sodden and unkind' makes explicit the normally implicit rejection of the urban, industrial – and northern – Britain from the image of 'England'. Where Drinkwater's poem breaks down – and I think it is a disastrous failure – is in his understandable, honest inability to reconcile this 'England' and its connotations, with modern life and its unrest – 'men bewildered in their travelling' – and with the war in particular. He compounds his problem by representing 'nature' as innocent and inert. The 'grazing flocks' drift like 'little clouds' across a 'windless sky': these sheep aren't real wool-bearers, potential lamb chops, just part of a visionary vista. What the third stanza is meant to suggest is hard to tell. 'Oaks' connote 'England' – 'hearts of oak', Royal Naval ships – but the 'world's adventure waiting in the pines' conveys to me nothing but the presumably irrelevant idea of Boy Scouts playing games in the woods. The night owls – actually vicious, efficient predators – 'purr' like domesticated cats.

ACTIVITY

What do the two poems by Drinkwater and de la Mare have in common?

DISCUSSION

Leaving the weakness of Drinkwater's rhetoric aside (de la Mare's seems to me to be much stronger), I would suggest that common to both poems are the following characteristics:

(a) A wish to locate value, quasi-religious significance, in *nature* – 'Buds ... with their *beauty*' (de la Mare), 'Dawns ... risen in *golden song*' (Drinkwater).

(b) This value is found not in complex natural processes (for example, owls commanding the food chain, sheep giving birth to lambs) but in *nature-as-spectacle*. 'Nature' is presented, even by de la Mare, in terms of broad, distant effects.

(c) Despite classical and biblical references, *English* 'nature' is always implicitly or explicitly the touchstone of 'beauty', of 'golden' value.

(d) But in each case English 'nature' is invested with melancholy – with the transience of the seasons, with threat (in 'Of Greatham'), with inevitable human death. England is viewed elegiacally. England is 'old', 'golden', spiritually potent – but infested with transience. *Nostalgia* is a dominant emotion.

2.7 Georgians exploit an element found in some major Romantic poems (Wordworth's 'The Solitary Reaper', Keats's 'Ode to a Nightingale'): the keen, but helpless emotion of nostalgia associated with a sense of all the human life which was faraway and is now dead, inaccessible to us – the pathos of *distance*. For the Romantics, these were emotions to be evoked powerfully and, occasionally, amid very different ones. A characteristic of much Georgianism is that it succumbs entirely and repeatedly to wistfulness and nostalgia.

ACTIVITY

Please now read, in the Poetry Anthology, Edward Thomas's 'Adlestrop'. Does this also exemplify such emotion?

DISCUSSION

Surely you had to say *yes*? Thomas's much anthologized poem has a vivid particularity which Drinkwater lacks. 'The steam hissed. Someone cleared his throat' – this line exemplifies 'Georgianism' at its best, if you like, appealing directly to experience that most readers would have been able to recall, making the ordinary significant and even haunting. But the 'stillness' of the haycocks and their 'fairness' match the 'high cloudlets in the sky' which correspond, 'nature-as-spectacle', to Drinkwater's 'little clouds that travel with no sound'. Again, the last two lines have a directness which Drinkwater can't give us – but play on almost exactly the same feeling as:

> From shire to shire the downs out of the dawn
> Were risen in golden song.

What is this feeling? It combines affirmation of 'England' – or at least of the southern English 'shires' – with *distance*, a wistful sense of life stretching away unknown, of something missed. 'Adlestrop', like 'Of Greatham', is about memory of *past* 'stillness', of *past* bird song. It is, less explicitly, nostalgic. (And at its weakest moment it virtually plagiarizes a major Romantic poet: Wordsworth, in 'Daffodils' had wandered *lonely* as a cloud, and had described his 'Lucy' in other poems as '*fair* as a star, when *only one* is shining in the sky'.)

2.8 What both Thomas and Drinkwater seem to represent is a crisis of English consciousness of 'England', mounting before the Great War, then exacerbated by that calamity. (The two poems were written within months of each other.) Both construct 'England' in terms of rusticity. Both are outsiders in actual rustic settings. Their love of the countryside, baffled by distance from it, expresses 'England' in terms of nostalgia. It's important now to consider the social setting, in town and country, from which they wrote.

The social background

2.9 'Of Greatham' and 'Adlestrop' evoke countryside almost devoid of human activity. This can partly be attributed to social–historical fact. Industrialization, from the eighteenth century, had promoted a drift to large and growing centres of population (by 1851 most British people lived in towns), and 'enclosures' of agricultural land deprived agricultural workers of ancient communal rights and helped to drive many away.

2.10 Meanwhile, the position of the agricultural labourer and the rural craftsman had become increasingly desperate. Ironically, it was the grey, windy North, so little celebrated by poets, that gave rural Englishmen the best rewards. Everywhere south of Derbyshire, 'the average earnings of ordinary labourers were below the poverty line'. Small wonder that men emigrated to Canada in large numbers, and that many others cycled off to work in nearby towns, where new industries might have lodged. War service in 1914–18 must actually have given some such men a sense of having an easier and more prosperous life.

2.11 The old crafts of country towns and villages were in terminal decay. Shoemakers and tailors could not compete with mass-produced goods, nor blacksmiths and wheelwrights with the big specialist producers of agricultural machinery. (For all this and more background, see Horn, 1984, pp.3–15.) So the rural 'England' which Thomas and Drinkwater looked out upon was one of decaying traditions and dwindling agricultural population. The process whereby the English 'South Country' would be transformed into a vast network of suburbs (which continues today with the proliferation of 'Greenfield Sites') was already fairly well advanced. The Home Counties around London were an arena where city workers found nests from which to commute, or sought weekend cottages. 'Inevitably', a historian comments, 'many of the "incomers" brought with them an idealised view of rural life, seeing it as a picturesque and peaceful backwater divorced from the hurly-burly of the urban world ... They also imported their own interests and values, which were often entirely different from those of the original inhabitants' (Horn, 1984, p.21). Cricket was a sport accorded almost transcendental status in this period. It was used to mask contradictions in harmonies – see the extracts from Neville Cardus's much admired writings in the Prose Anthology.

2.12 As the motor car became increasingly popular, England's 'green and pleasant' parts would be wholly accessible to the questing weekend tripper. The inter-war years, when the popularity of Georgian verses was at its height, were arguably the heyday of the 'English countryside' as *spectacle*. (TV4 *Crossing the Border* explores this point further.) Railway, bus and tube publicity incited city dwellers to head for fresh air. The Shell petrol company, in its famous advertisements, encapsulated a vision of pastoral England, available to the car owner. The cult of village cricket as the quintessential expression of English character was ritually celebrated. Motorways had yet to slash 'shires' to ribbons. Old inns still served real ale, under signs painted by rustic specialists. Horses still ploughed the land (though increasingly they were replaced by tractors), and so village blacksmiths still survived. The townee tripper, or Georgian-influenced poet, could fool himself that he was in touch with the real, immemorial 'England', with the countrymen of Chaucer and Shakespeare. In the Second World War, the myth that 'England' was still 'green and pleasant' would prove to have great value as a cement for national unity. Earlier rural reality had been direly annotated, however, by the country-bred novelist Winifred Holtby, in the mid-1930s:

> I remember a village with no artificial light, no telephone, no telegraph, no health insurance system, no means of transport except our own pony-trap and the weekly carrier's cart, with its slow horse which took an hour and a half to get to the nearest shop ... the babies that died unnecessarily and the rigid class divisions ... And then I think of today's raised wages, the improved housing, health services, buses...
>
> (quoted in Horn, 1984, p.233)

These improvements in comforts had arrived despite inter-war depression in agriculture which had left many areas looking desolate, with derelict fields, choked ditches, overgrown hedges, rotting fences, and decaying barns. (Auden describes such a landscape in one of the poems you will be reading in Section 4 of this block.)

Charlotte Mew and Edmund Blunden

2.13 We shall now consider two Georgian poems which confront rural life at closer quarters than 'Adlestrop' and 'Of Greatham'. What can these tell us about the construction of 'England'?

ACTIVITY

Please read 'The Farmer's Bride' by Charlotte Mew in the Poetry Anthology. Can we say that it serves to 'construct' an 'England', or to reinforce constructions made more explicitly elsewhere?

DISCUSSION

My answer would be that a reader of Georgian tastes would probably at once respond positively to its attempt to give voice to an 'authentic' agriculturalist and to its evocation of English landscapes. But even the most naive such reader would surely find the poem disturbing, 'destructive', rather than inspirational or nostalgic. The questions that it sets up about female sexuality and patriarchal authority pull the 'English yeoman', celebrated in other poems, out of the 'immemorial' past, out of 'tradition' – and into a field of controversy and doubt.

2.14 Not that the poem's mode is 'realistic', nor that 'realism' is its objective. Mew (1869–1928) was born, and committed suicide, in London. Her father was an architect. She moved in 'artistic' circles in the big city. Her reputation suddenly blossomed in 1916 when Harold Monro (a close ally of Edward Marsh) published 'The Farmer's Bride' as the title poem of her first 'slim volume'. Virginia Woolf regarded her as 'the greatest living poetess'. She was almost certainly lesbian in leaning, but 'there is no sign in her work that Charlotte Mew accepted her sexuality' (Warner, 1981). What makes 'The Farmer's Bride' such a remarkable poem is the refraction of unconventional sexuality through a Hardyesque, Georgian medium. The use of dialect recalls Hardy.

2.15 The woman is assimilated with 'nature' in a way that recalls a standard Georgian motif borrowed from the Romantics. She seems to be in communication with 'birds and rabbits' and 'beasts in stall'. She recalls Wordsworth's 'Lucy' and Keats's 'Meg Merrilies', and has that in common with country folk wheeled on by Georgian writers to represent the Enduring Spirit of English Tradition. But her 'wildness' is not the Boy Scout wildness of Drinkwater, not like the freedom of tramps and charcoal burners and gypsies celebrated elsewhere in Georgian verse. It is alien to human conviviality. The farmer–speaker, her husband, compares her to a 'little frightened fay'. It would be reassuring, in terms of 'Englishness' if she *were* a fairy, like one of Shakespeare's. She is something more problematical – a human being behaving as if mad. The puzzlement of the farmer–speaker, his admiration for her beauty, represent decent normality confronted with a force which it can't understand or cope with. The last stanza seems to me to convey thwarted sexual attraction with exceptional power.

2.16 I wish I had space to discuss the brilliance of the poem's technique – its disturbing mixture of prosaic lines loose in their rhythm with taut quatrains and couplets, its great metrical variety kept under unobtrusive control. But I hope I've said enough to suggest that a poem may be generically Georgian, and be by a 'townee' about the countryside, without slumping into cosiness or wistfulness.

BLOCK 3
'ENGLISHNESS'

2.17   Edmund Blunden (1896–1974) was a Georgian poet whose reputation has remained steady. Perhaps one reason why his evocations of country life have always been acceptable is that he himself was truly a countryman, brought up in rural Kent, the son of a schoolmaster. (Though plenty of countrymen have written dreadful verse!) Even when, as in his prose work *Cricket Country* (1943), Blunden is most obviously 'constructing England', he is doing so out of materials easily familiar to him.

ACTIVITY

Please now read his early poem 'The Barn', in the Poetry Anthology. Thinking back to our discussion of Drinkwater, how would you express the contrast?

DISCUSSION

Crucially, this carefully made, accurately detailed poem is *demystifying* the countryside which Drinkwater, and even Thomas, mystify and mist over.

2.18   The poem begins as if it will be a prime expression of Georgian nostalgia. The barn is in poor repair, dark and dirty, defaced with graffiti. But the third stanza defies wistful thoughts. The barn still serves its purpose. It is 'old and very old' – as old, one might think, as de la Mare's English 'nature'. But it is full of 'blithe cheerful noise'. What Blunden is affirming, at the time of the Great War, is a faith in the continuity of English country practices. 'Wane' and 'change' are not a threat. So the poem *is* reassuring, and might seem cosy. Some of its adjectives are weakly conventional –'merry', 'blithe'. But the poem is essentially sturdy – not challenging, but not naive or posturing. Such detailed description had actually been quite rare in English verse, and Blunden's freshness is due, I think, to genuine originality.

Edward Thomas

2.19   Much of Edward Thomas also remains fresh for readers. But his 'Englishness' is highly problematic, as we shall now see.

2.20   Thomas, for a start, was born to Welsh parents in London and always regarded himself as Welsh. Welsh critics celebrate him as a Welsh poet. He represents the process whereby 'Englishness' was redefined, from the eighteenth century, largely by non-English subjects of the United Kingdom interested in creating an English or British identity which could include themselves: by such bestselling Scots as James ('Rule Britannia') Thomson, Walter Scott in *Ivanhoe*, Thomas Carlyle, Samuel Smiles, John Buchan, Conan Doyle – and by the Irish dramatists Goldsmith, Sheridan, Wilde and Shaw.

2.21   Thomas's 'accidental cockney nativity', as he called his own birth in 1878, followed his father's migration from Tredegar to a clerical job connected with railways in London. The poet grew up in Clapham, a suburb then still close to the Surrey countryside. Stan Smith, in his sympathetic study, *Edward Thomas*, observes:

> That he could himself embrace his Welshness and yet at the same time not feel the strain of reconciling it with his idea of England testifies to the power of ideology to contain contradictions. Yet the strain is apparent everywhere in his work, focused most acutely in that sense of perpetual exile which pervades his poetry...

The play between London birth and Welsh allegiance is the key to understanding the idea of England in Thomas' work. For the two extremes open up that expanse of countryside which stretches between them as a third, *ideological* terrain, the perpetually disappearing heart of a lost unity and wholeness which has in fact always been an *imaginary* plenitude, a utopian land of lost content which is precisely nowhere.

(Smith, 1986, pp.15,19)

ACTIVITY

Adlestrop lies between London and Wales. Now re-read that poem, considering whether it suits Smith's argument?

DISCUSSION

I'd say it supports Smith's case very well. Adlestrop offers a vision of contentment – flowers, birds, haycocks, clouds – which is, in effect, 'precisely nowhere'. 'No one left and no one came … still and lonely fair' – the vision is transient, empty of human presence. Adlestrop is 'only' a 'name'. Just as Thomas was born in London by accident, so it's an accident that the train, 'unwontedly', stops here.

2.22   Thomas had struggled to support a growing family by incessant literary hackwork. Perhaps it was 'accident' which released his poetry after years of writing book reviews, personal essays, critical studies, and works about the countryside, an example of which you met in Section 1. He met the American poet Robert Frost in October 1913. Between then and his death at the front in France in April 1917 he wrote all his poetry, with Frost's encouragement.

2.23   Politically, the years of his adult life were turbulent. Thomas was drawn to the romantic socialism of William Morris. He admired contemporary pioneers of trade unionism, and had no sympathy for the landlords who actually possessed the English countryside about which he wrote. Being Welsh enhanced his sense that England was a country stolen from its people: the Welsh descended from ancient Britons conquered by Anglo-Saxons. Look at this remarkable poem 'The Combe' – very far from cosy:

The Combe
The Combe was ever dark, ancient and dark,
Its mouth is stopped with bramble, thorn, and briar;
And no one scrambles over the sliding chalk
By beech and yew and perishing juniper
Down the half precipices of its sides, with roots
And rabbit holes for steps. The sun of Winter,
The moon of Summer, and all the singing birds
Except the missel-thrush that loves juniper,
Are quite shut out. But far more ancient and dark
The Combe looks since they killed the badger there,
Dug him out and gave him to the hounds,
That most ancient Briton of English beasts.

Elsewhere, Thomas's speaker is aware of being shut out from that dark core of English Britishness which 'The Combe' represents.

2.24   Please now read 'The Penny Whistle' in the Poetry Anthology. There is a piquant discrepancy – I think it's this detail that above all makes the poem original and interesting – between the 'white' letter which the girl is reading and the occupational blackness of her and her brother. The word *black* is of crucial importance in the poem. 'Ghylls' here refers, I think, to the 'radiating plates arranged vertically on the underside of the cap or pileus of fungi'. Any large shop mushroom will show you how this fits well with the image of branching trees, 'blackened' because rendered leafless by winter, 'blackened anew' (this is subtle observation) by the very brightness of the moon which emphasizes by contrast their darkness. The brooks have 'black hollow' voices. Like 'The Combe' they are at odds with sun and moon. The 'moon–white'/ 'nature–black' opposition is carried forward into human life. Charcoal burning is a very ancient occupation associated with the smelting of iron, carried on long before the Saxons came. 'Old hearths' carries a charge that we've seen is typically Georgian, emphasizing the depth of tradition in the English landscape. They are not incompatible with fresh springtime renewal, 'fresh primroses'. The charcoal burners are curiously like 'incomers' into this terrain. The white linen links them with respectability. The letter suggests ample contact with the contemporary world of posts and commerce. From this, the male charcoal burner has, as it were, retreated into a 'thicket' (compare, again, 'The Combe'). The 'old nursery melody' which he plays on his whistle expresses something that words cannot express.

2.25   In childhood, we are, the poem suggests, instinctively in touch with the 'black', secret, suppressed yet defiant ancestral spirit of the land which was British before it was English. The whistle recreates a truth felt by children (for Thomas, present in the Welsh songs which his family taught him) which an adult's words cannot encompass.

2.26   'Old Man', a much more searching poem – I think it's Thomas's masterpiece – also confronts the business of 'naming'. When Adam in Eden (according to Genesis) named the beasts, he must have chosen the words himself. His word for 'lion' was, presumably, his own, not English 'lion', Italian 'leone', Swahili 'simba'. Through the power to name, people in different cultures express the different distinctions they draw between phenomena, and between ideas and emotions resulting from contact with them. In 'The Penny Whistle' Thomas's speaker cannot *name*, find *names* to encompass the meaning conveyed by the music.

2.27   Please now read 'Old Man' in the Poetry Anthology, thinking about the business of naming. The little bush in the poem, 'Old Man', is not 'Old Man's Beard'. *Chambers Twentieth Century Dictionary* obligingly defines 'Old Man' as 'a southernwood', and the *Oxford English Dictionary* describes this as 'a hardy deciduous shrub, *Artemisia abrotanum*, having a fragrant aromatic smell and a sour taste, originally native to the south of Europe, and formerly much cultivated for medicinal purposes'. The native 'Old Man's Beard' (*Clematis vitalba*) turns up in another Thomas poem, 'Lob'.

2.28   This is a key poem in regard to 'Englishness' in Thomas, but too long to be discussed in this block. Lob is a figure who represents archetypal, immemorial, common-man Englishness. He was the man who called

> The wild cherry tree the merry tree,
> The rose campion Bridget-in-her-bravery;
> And in a tender mood he, as I guess,
> Christened one flower Love-in-idleness,
> And while he walked from Exeter to Leeds
> One April called all cuckoo-flowers Milkmaids.

Lob is the genius of the language as well as of the folk and the countryside. The painful truth is that language is shifting. Language is not 'natural', or 'God-given' – it changes as populations change. In 'Old Man' Thomas, naming, attempting to name, explores below the surface of Englishness, reaching into primal experience, but not attaining any vision of Eden. The capacity to name, to find words for experience, is in fact part of adult pain, adult alienation.

2.29 The contradictory names given to *Artemisia abrotanum* correspond to its ambiguous appearance: 'hoar-green'. 'Hoar' denotes frost and connotes old age, 'green' connotes spring and youth, 'Lad's Love'. The wonderfully managed, brooding, circling 'voice' of the opening – Thomas handles virtually free verse here with a relaxed mastery characteristic of his best work – expresses despair of words alongside pleasure in them. The 'thing', the plant itself, 'clings not to the names in spite of time. And yet I like the names.' The purpose of names is to discriminate, differentiate. These names fail in their essential function. They are, in philosophical usage, 'accidental'; they do not connect with the 'substance', the quiddity, the 'thing'. Words are just 'things by themselves', we infer – and Thomas connects here with a Modernist preoccupation (see Block 2). As you will see, similar preoccupations can be found in Caribbean writers (Derek Walcott, Block 6) and women writers (Block 7).

2.30 The second paragraph opens with an apparently firm discrimination, between 'liking' and 'love'. But to say that one 'loves' something one doesn't like is to give 'love' an unusual definition. It seems to be an adult emotion, one that the child can only grow into: it is, say, the feeling that binds a man to his wife even after easy affection is dead.

2.31 The child un-naming ('not a word she says…') seems to experience the bush directly, 'thinking, perhaps, of nothing', as in Eden Eve tasted forbidden fruit. As God forbade Eve to pick that, so the speaker of the poem forbids his daughter. Why? Her constant 'plucking' of the bush stunts it, he suggests. But on a symbolic level, the forbidding suggests that the father doesn't want his child to lapse from Eden into the 'knowledge of good and evil', the wisdom and agony of adulthood, which the bush represents. Its names denote a span of experience from young love to old age, but these categories in themselves are inadequate to convey the bitterness of grown experience continuous between twenty and seventy. Or is the point that the speaker 'knows' neither – a possible reading of the second line? He is past first youth, not yet old; the 'bitterness' of the plant is like that of disillusion without the reputed fulfilment of old age.

2.32 In any case, the speaker is haunted, sniffing the plant, by a (primal) memory which he cannot name, cannot describe. His consciousness conveys to him only an image of transition – 'an avenue, dark, nameless, without end' – and a sense of total isolation. That is the unnameable core of experience.

2.33 Thomas's vision excludes Christianity or any other religious consolation. In this he was typical of his freethinking generation. His quest for England is therefore a quest for an alternative source of spiritual validation. When war came in 1914, he despised jingoistic cries and slogans, yet came to feel that he must fight for 'England' in this crisis; combat was a spiritual necessity.

ACTIVITY

Please now read 'As the team's head brass' in the Poetry Anthology, and this time read the poem aloud. So far I have said almost nothing about Thomas's technique. But the 'voice' that he creates in his poems is a crucial element in their content, and their 'Englishness'. Rhythmic devices establish this voice. Note down a few points about his technique here which strike you.

DISCUSSION

My points are these:

Thomas uses 'blank verse', and the metrical 'norm' which we sense in the poem is that of the commonest metre in English, the iambic pentameter as used in famous blank verse by Shakespeare, Wordsworth, Tennyson, Browning and many others.

> As the team's head brass flashed out on the turn
> The lovers disappeared into the wood...
>
> To be or not to be, that is the question –
> Whether tis nobler in the mind to suffer...
>
> There was a Boy, ye knew him well, ye cliffs
> And islands of Winander. Many a time...

The examples from Shakespeare and Wordsworth show that Thomas, in his opening, was perfectly orthodox in introducing variations to the basic five-stress, iambic pattern. An iamb consists of an unstressed followed by a stressed syllable, 'To bé', 'The lóvers'. A pentameter has five stresses, hence the 'blank verse' line normally has ten syllables. But a purely mechanical application of the norm would almost certainly be poor verse. While we keep it in our heads, are aware of it as the underlying formal basis, our ear gratefully accepts variations. Thus the second line of Hamlet's soliloquy opens with a trochee (stressed/unstressed). Since we will not in practice stress 'of' when reading Wordsworth's second line aloud, that effectually has only four feet. And so on ...

But Thomas goes on to introduce variations which take us far from the underlying norm.

> I sat among the boughs of the fallen elm
> That strewed an angle of the fallow, and
> Watched the plough narrowing a yellow square
> Of charlock...

This is blank verse dissolving into the rhythms of prose – or of conversation (though given intensity by assonance – 'fall', 'fallow', 'narrowing', 'yellow'). The poem's third line has eleven syllables. The slackening that results prepares us for line four, where we could only find five stresses if, artificially, we emphasized 'of' and 'and'. The run-overs 'and /Watched', 'square /Of' help create the illusion that what we are getting from Thomas is close to intimate speech – tentative, half formed. When the speaker actually exchanges words with the ploughman, the rhythm becomes extremely loose.

> 'Have you been out?' 'No.' 'And don't want to, perhaps?'

There are six stresses at least – seven if we stress 'don't'. Counting syllables and finding stresses is not always the most important thing to do when one is trying to understand poetry. But here the mixture of 'normal' lines –

> In France they killed him. It was back in March,

is a completely orthodox iambic pentameter – with others of apparently casual looseness *is* highly significant. We are satisfied by the former that Thomas's utterance is under control, beguiled by the latter into believing that this is a 'real-life' incident honestly recorded and conveyed to us conversationally. John Lucas has written of 'Old Man' that its lines 'have the slow, patient, exquisitely honest movement of a mind brooding long' (1986, p.85). Similar technical means in 'As the team's head brass' produce the effect of 'exquisitely honest' immediacy. We do not want to believe that Thomas *invented* this scene, this conversation. It would shock us, as if we'd discovered a good friend to be a liar.

This effect of honesty was as important in Thomas's 'Englishness' as a similar effect would be in George Orwell's. We are lured by it to identify ourselves with England as if this were the natural, the obvious thing to do, whereas patriotic tub-thumping or stilted romantic rhetoric might alienate, even amuse us. This poem's projection of 'Englishness' is stoical at best, fearful at worst.

The wood into which the lovers disappear is like 'The Combe', and the thicket in 'The Penny Whistle', a place of refuge from 'civilization'. John Lucas argues that the elm on which the poem's speaker sits had become 'an unofficial symbol of (southern) England at this period' (1986, p.91). Whether we sense this symbolism or not, the fact that it has fallen in a blizzard on the very night that the ploughman's mate was killed in the war emphasizes the threat at this moment to English rusticity. Men are being lost, won't come back – who will shift the fallen tree? Who will plant new elms? The speaker is despondent, or uncertain. He first says he would 'want' to fight in France if only he could come back, then speculates about a 'Blighty' wound – losing an arm would get him out of the war – then grimly puns that if he lost his head he would 'want nothing more'. (Being dead would mean no more wanting; but his remark could also be construed as meaning that he would like to be dead. Losing one's head could mean: (a) having it blown off; (b) losing control of oneself in battle; (c) perhaps, also, going mad.) It is only accident – the simultaneous fallings of tree and ploughman's mate – that enables him to sit here, yet this accident represents a transition from one world to another. The ploughman suggests that the old world was better, yet at once expresses a tentative hope that divine providence makes sense of the war. And of the destruction of 'England'? 'For the last time', in the third line from the end, has three layers of suggestion:

> *literally* – the speaker gets up and goes away;
>
> *by implication* – he will go to France, fight and die so this is the last time he will see English ploughing;
>
> *symbolically* – horse-ploughing itself is doomed, finished; the team is 'stumbling', mechanization will replace it.

2.34 The very 'honesty' that makes Thomas's construction of 'England' so compelling helps to undermine faith in 'England's' capacity to survive. So it is not surprising that we find other poems in which Thomas – a devoted patriot in time of war – seems to struggle to overcome a personal melancholy associated with transition, decay and loss, and to affirm an enduring, eternal England. See, for instance, 'Haymaking' in the Poetry Anthology. Edna Longley (1986) praises its 'concreteness and empiricism'. I find it deeply unconvincing, even off-putting. What do you think?

In the next section of this block, I shall be considering how P.G. Wodehouse constructed a very different version of Englishness for a different kind of reader.

3 P.G. Wodehouse: 'Indian Summer of an Uncle'

Why 'Jeeves'?

3.1 Well, *why*, in a course like this, should we 'study' Jeeves? Throughout 'Plum' Wodehouse's very long life (1881–1975) and immensely prolific career, he never showed any sign of wanting to write enduring 'literature'. His published correspondence (*Performing Flea*, 1953) reveals that he worried a great deal about his plots and other mechanics of his fiction, not at all about what emotions or ideas it might or should convey. He was fulsomely praised by gifted fellow writers – by Evelyn Waugh above all – but he distanced himself from 'intellectual' life. He was clearly more at home in the world of the Broadway musical. He collaborated as lyricist with such master composers as Kern and Gershwin. As an acknowledged innovator on Broadway, he would be a figure of considerable interest in cultural history if he had never written a comic story or created Jeeves.

3.2 When *Very Good, Jeeves!* was published in 1930, Wodehouse was enjoying a lucrative stint as a Hollywood script writer. In this phase of his career, he was averaging about £100,000 a year from freelance writing (worth millions today). His life centred completely on his writing and he produced story after story to satisfy a known public demand. He had found that the public in America liked Jeeves, whom he had first offered to it in 1917. In his stories Wodehouse aimed simply to entertain, and he saw no reason to be ashamed of this. As a vastly successful 'formula' writer he had hit on, with Jeeves and Bertie, 'formula' characters as appealing as Holmes and Watson, James Bond and Rumpole.

3.3 'Perfection, of a kind, was what he was after', Auden wrote in 'Epitaph on a Tyrant' (1939). Like any master of formula comedy, Wodehouse drives his invented figments of humanity despotically towards a 'happy ending'; and there is a consonance between the myths of authoritarian politics and the basis of fantasizing comedy. We enjoy in Wodehouse the suspense engendered by plots which we know *must be resolved* to our satisfaction: for Mussolini or Stalin, unhappy endings are unthinkable. Art must be 'optimistic'. The poise of the Wooster world, disrupted by an imperious aunt or a presumptuous fellow-Drone down on his luck and appealing, never in vain, to the 'Code of the Woosters', will, at the story's end, have been restored, if necessary by precipitate flight from the scene to some place of safety. Of course, where Wodehouse's notion of perfection differs utterly from Hitler's is that pomposity, arrogance and cruelty *always lose*.

Reading Jeeves

3.4 Now read 'Indian Summer of an Uncle' in the Prose Anthology. Please try, if you can can, to clear your mind of all preconceptions as you read, or re-read, this story. It is a solecism to suppose that Jeeves is an archetypal English *butler*. He is *not* that. What, in fact, or rather in fiction, *is* he? It is conventional to say that Bertie is a 'silly ass'. Please test this judgement as you read. Does it stand up? And was George Orwell right when he argued 'In defence of P.G. Wodehouse' (in 1945, after the notorious Berlin broadcasts made when the author was a prisoner of the Nazis) that Wodehouse had invented and stuck to a pre-First World War vision of England – 'naive, traditional and, at bottom, admiring' – which took no account of politics or any other historical developments (Orwell and Angus, 1968, pp.396–8)? Is

Jeeves really, as Hilaire Belloc argued in the 1930s, 'the living image ... of the English character in action?' (quoted in Usborne, 1976, p.214). With an open mind, please, consider these and also the following more specific questions.

Language and discourse

3.5 How does Bertie, as first-person narrator, 'position' you, as his reader? On what terms do you have to be with him if you are to enter into his story? You may dislike his voice. If so, please grit your teeth (the story isn't long) and note the specific features of Bertie's discourse that repel you.

3.6 You will have your attention drawn to some quotations from famous literature. There may be others you won't spot. One obvious function of these is to characterize Jeeves as well-read. No credit for spotting that! But our narrator is not Jeeves but Bertie. How does the bombardment of quotations modify our reading of Bertie, not as a 'character', but as a *writer*, which, according to convention, we must assume him to be?

3.7 Language, in speech and in literature, exists for us in many different registers, dialects and jargons. How does Bertie's compare and contrast with those of other characters in the story?

Gender and power

3.8 How can you describe the Jeeves/Wooster relationship in terms of these categories? Firstly, *power* – who is in control? Secondly *class* – who, by what tokens, has higher social status? Thirdly – this may surprise you – *gender*. If this were a male–female relationship, what sort of relationship would it be like? Mother–son? Brother–sister? Husband–wife? Lover–mistress?

3.9 And in relation to the foregoing, how do *aunts* figure in the Wooster world, in terms of *power* and in relation to *gender*?

Englishness

3.10 Now, 'England' and 'Englishness'. What vision of 'England' is conveyed in these stories? Is it purely conventional, or does it contain elements of fresh observation? If Belloc is right, that Jeeves is somehow quintessentially 'English', what features does 'Englishness' have?

3.11 It's worth introducing a well-known quotation from Stanley Baldwin's best-selling book, *On England* (1937). Baldwin – so loathed by Miss Jean Brodie (see Block 4) – was twice prime minister between the wars, first as a Conservative (1924–29), then at the front of a National Coalition (1935–37). This is the despised National Government that is referred to in TV5 *Left and Write* by Julian Symons. His stolid, tolerant, pipe-smoking image made him one of the representative 'Englishmen' of his day. (He hated, he said, the term 'Britain' – 'When God wants a hard thing done, He tells it', not to His Britons, but 'to His Englishmen'.) Baldwin said, in 1924:

> To me England is the country, and the country is England ... The sounds of England, the tinkle of the hammer on the anvil of the country smithy ... that wood smoke that our ancestors, tens of thousands of years ago, must have caught on the air when they were coming home with the result of the day's forage, when they were still nomads, and when they were still roaming the forests and the plains of the continent of Europe. [!!!] These things strike down into the very depths of our nature ... These are the things that make England...
>
> (Baldwin, 1937, pp.11,16–17)

3.12 You will find it easy enough to relate the foregoing to the characteristic nostalgia of Georgian poetry, discussed already in this block. You may also, if you know some twentieth-century history, see at once how Baldwin's 'blood and soil' racist rhetoric was characteristic of a tendency in nationalisms all

3 P.G. WODEHOUSE: 'INDIAN SUMMER OF AN UNCLE'

over Europe, expressed in music, sculpture and painting as well as by politicians, which reached a hideous climax in the culture of German National Socialism. But my question to you now is: *granted* that this is the rhetoric of dominant ideology, of power, and *granted* that you've seen how a subtle Georgian, Edward Thomas, exposed and raised questions about contradictions within this rhetoric in some poems, while accepting its structure in others – well, where does 'Plum' Wodehouse and the language he gives to Bertie Wooster stand in relationship to it? *Could* Bertie, or Jeeves, utter anything like that?

Language and discourse

3.13   Whether you feel included or not, Bertie assumes that you are a pal of his. The opening of 'Indian Summer of an Uncle' assumes that the reader knows, or can infer, that 'the Drones' is a London club. The convention, in these stories at any rate, operates *as if* he was talking to us.

3.14   But who, 'if you know what I mean', are 'we'? If you reject Bertie's assumption of friendship it may be because you are a serious-minded person and your literature-reading self is outraged by his inane facetiousness. If you accept it, play his game, this entails ignoring the impulses which might make you rush away as quickly as possible from a real-life Bertie, and going along with his way of talking and his view of the world.

3.15   To rephrase my opening question: as a *critic*, how do you assess the character of the game you are playing with Bertie as you connive at his way of addressing you – what is expected of you, how do you measure up?

3.16   The demands are heavier than you might think. An 'ideal' Wooster-reader requires:

(a)   a feeling for the nuances of various sorts of slang;

(b)   a capacity to recognize fictional, poetic and journalistic clichés;

(c)   the ability to delight in the clash of different slangs, registers and jargons;

(d)   some alertness to the details of English society in the period 1880–1930 (during Wodehouse's lifetime).

3.17   What all this implies is that Bertie himself is a very deft user of language. He is at ease with French. In 'Indian Summer of an Uncle', we have: *noblesse* (p.28); *grande dame ... régime* (p.30); *joie de vivre* (p.32); *mésalliance* (p.38); and *distrait* (p.40) – all correctly employed. He is, furthermore, fluent with such Americanisms as 'ball of fire' (p.37), 'buddies' (p.39), 'it is the goods' (p.42). His own basic *argot*, dialect, 'if you know what I mean', is an upper and upper-middle class English, larded with such expressions as 'tooled off', 'buzzed off', 'binge', 'dash it', 'shook the onion'. The noted American critic Edmund Wilson once remarked that the USA had been pervaded by a kind of 'Anglo-American jargon in the insouciant British tradition, which I believe to be mainly the creation of the Englishman P.G. Wodehouse' (quoted in Green, 1983, p.237). This indicates how hard it can be to pin down the territorial range, or even origins, of a given 'slang' expression in the twentieth century. But Bertie's spoken discourse clearly suggests upper-class English enriched with up-to-date Americanisms.

3.18   But Wooster's vocabulary is not limited to this idiom. Far from it. A word which may have struck you is 'volplaned' (p.29). This refers to an aeroplane gliding to earth with its engine shut off, and must have been a recent usage in 1930. From the context we can infer that it is not used as standard 'slang' – like 'legged it', which immediately proceeds it – but as *mot juste*, as Jeeves would put it. It provides an amusingly exact simile for the stately swoop of a genteel lady into a chair, all the more amusing because of its conflict with 'legged it' which does not suggest stateliness at all. Bertie is prone to mix discourses like this. Is the effect rather like malapropism – an absurd tongue-bungling suited to a silly ass? Or does it suggest wit, on Bertie's part, aimed at producing comic bathos? The fact that it isn't always easy to tell points us, I think, to a key feature of Wooster's creation of Bertie through language.

3.19   Evelyn Waugh, asked once why he so admired Wodehouse, replied, 'One has to regard a man as a Master who can produce on average three uniquely brilliant and entirely original similes on every page' (quoted in Donaldson, 1982, p.5). I think my own pick from this story would be 'I heard Aunt Agatha rumble like a volcano just before it starts to set about the neighbours' (p.36). Such jokes – characteristic of Bertie/Wodehouse – depend on quick-silver interchange between the sublime and the ridiculous. A volcano is awesome, but setting about the neighbours is what people do in vulgar suburbs. Like so much successful humour, Wodehouse's is irreverent. And we owe his simile here to the voice of Bertram Wooster. Undoubtedly, he has been trained to impersonate his creator, Wodehouse, but his gift of mimicry is in itself god-like. Bertie is *cleverly amusing*.

3.20   But what of the god-like Jeeves? His use of English, by contrast, is limited to one register. It is correct, polite, formal, pompous and carefully literal:

> 'Contracting a matrimonial alliance, sir.'
>
> 'Good Lord! Did he tell you?'
>
> 'No, sir. Oddly enough, I chance to be acquainted with the other party in the matter.'
>
> (Prose Anthology, p.27)

It is essential to Jeeves as a fictional conception that he should *always* be *formally* respectful and meticulous in his language.

3.21   He is, furthermore, the source of most of the literary quotations which slip in and out of his employer's discourse. You will not have missed, in 'Indian Summer of an Uncle', the poet Burns (p.28), the 'Swan of Avon' (p.37) Tennyson, and Shakespeare again (p.42). There are many more quotations in the two stories. It has to be conceded that Jeeves's range of reference does not extend much, if at all, beyond the works of Shakespeare and standard 'anthology pieces' favoured by editors of the young Wodehouse's era. Bertie, meanwhile, is saturated in the clichés of romantic fiction and of journalism.

3.22   What effects are produced by this allusiveness? Chiefly, I think, it contributes to effects of comic discrepancy (like the volcano/neighbours juxtaposition cited above). Lofty lines – banal or ridiculous happenings.

3.23   To conclude this section: language in this story, *except for Jeeves's*, is highly unstable. A great deal of its humour depends on comic discrepancy between different discourses invoked. So far from being confined to the jargon of a brainless young clubman, Bertie skids and stumbles – but also (knowingly?) *swoops* – between one level of language and another. He is (has to be) endowed with all the gifts of his creator, Wodehouse, even if, 'playing the game' with him, we are often led to infer that his surprising verbal felicities are the result of blunder, bad taste, or accident. Jeeves, by contrast, is unerring, but limited.

Gender, power and aunts

3.24   What is the precise position of Jeeves? He is a 'personal gentleman's gentleman', like his young friend Smethurst (p.37). He is not a domestic servant, though he makes Bertie's breakfast and brings it to him in bed. He is not a butler, though he carries in drinks. He is more than a valet, though he looks after and, as need arises, packs up Bertie's belongings ('Pack the toothbrush', p.29). He is regarded by Aunt Agatha, it seems, as a 'menial' (p.36). His status depends on his master's (hence the cold vindictiveness he displays in certain stories when Bertie's choice of clothes offends his own sense of sartorial propriety). On the other hand, he is given ample scope to settle matters his own way.

3.25 Bertie treats him on occasions like an equal. Their agreement at the end of 'Indian Summer of an Uncle' that flight from Aunt Agatha is essential is sealed by Bertie for once producing, Jeeves-like, a quotation from Shakespeare, though one that exposes his relative frivolity. He is capable, when disconcerted by Jeeves, of assuming (as on p.41) what he takes to be the 'cold, level voice' of authority, employer to servant. Interestingly, at this point his language – 'All this is a direct consequence of your scheme' – becomes, briefly, as formal as Jeeves's own. The idea that Servant may be far more than equal to Master in most or all practical respects is an old one in comedy – Beaumarchais' Figaro is a famous example and there was a play very popular in Wodehouse's youth and heyday, James Barrie's *The Admirable Crichton*, which used it.

3.26 That said, suppose Jeeves and Wooster were male and female. What sort of relationship would we call it? Father–daughter? Hardly. Brother and sister? No – they do not have origins and childhood in common. Man and wife? Mother and son? Here, surely, we are on to something. We can imagine the whole canon translated into the terms of either of these relationships, if Bertie becomes the headstrong, vulnerable son or husband and Jeeves the Wise Wife or Mother Who Knows Best. Bertie constantly overrates his own ability to fix things. He attributes to himself a 'lynx eye' (p.26), takes a 'firm line' (p.35) and considers himself benevolent in treating Jeeves like a 'counsellor without equal' (p.41). In the end it is Jeeves, mother-like, wife-like, who sorts things out.

3.27 In that case, *Who is Father*? In early twentieth-century Western culture, authority – social, political, moral – was firmly vested in men. The vote for all adult women in Britain antedated these stories by only a couple of years. Where, in 'Indian Summer of an Uncle', do we find a centre of male authority corresponding to that in 'real' society?

3.28 Two answers are possible:

(a) Jeeves – but Jeeves *is* a servant and he *does* side with Bertie...

(b) Nowhere. Older upper and upper middle-class English men in Wodehouse's fiction fall into three categories. There are wealthy fools and eccentrics, like Lord Emsworth of Blandings. There are other well-off men who are bullies, pompous asses, cheats, MPs and, worst of all, magistrates, who fine members of the Drones, or even send them to prison, for sporting seizures of policemen's helmets. These are always confounded, defeated, and made ridiculous. Finally, there are jolly old souls who were naughty in the Naughty Nineties. Uncle George, in 'Indian Summer of an Uncle', is a hybrid – part naughty, part fool.

3.29 In the Wooster world power is concentrated in aunts. Agatha epitomizes aunthood as a centre of oppression. She is censorious of Bertie's habits, his idleness, his drinking. She is prone to insist that he does something, for once, for his family. Still worse, she is liable to decide that he should get married. Though Bertie is of adult years and has comfortable independent means, he cannot overtly defy her: he can only obey, out-manoeuvre her, or flee from her dread purlieux (as at the end of 'Indian Summer of an Uncle'). In a later Jeeves book, *The Mating Season*, she is credited with wearing barbed wire next to the skin and eating broken bottles.

In that story, Jeeves and Bertie help the hapless Haddock, Squire of Deverill Hall, to burst free from a 'surging sea of aunts', no less than five, all living with him.

ACTIVITY

What significance can we attach to this aunt-obsession?

DISCUSSION

Biographers dabbling in psychology point to Wodehouse's own early life as the probable source of Bertie's aunt-phobia. Wodehouse *père* had been a colonial civil servant in the East. 'Plum', like his brothers, had been sent to private schools in England as a boarder and farmed out in holiday times to the care of assorted aunts. In Wodehouse's case, separation from parental love seems to have had three effects which he rendered harmless: as a child he got on better with servants than with grown people of his own class; he regarded older relatives with fear and suspicion; and he was utterly devoted to the public school, Dulwich College, which he attended with great success, playing cricket and rugby for the school's first teams. The original of Aunt Agatha is Wodehouse's Aunt Mary, who harried and harassed him for his own good.

But as Richard Usborne acutely points out, 'A monstrous aunt can be funny. A monstrous mother would be tragic' (1976, p.43). Aunt Agatha is more an Aunt Sally than a monster of evil. Considering her as a surrogate for patriarchal authority in society, she reminds me of figures in inter-war public life who were risible rather than terrifying (Baldwin's ridiculous Home Secretary, Joynson-Hicks, for instance, a Low Church Anglican, who zealously persecuted such 'obscene' artists as D.H. Lawrence).

The crack against Aunt Agatha which Bertie risks over the phone (p.41) is evidence that he is not, I contend, 'the super-fool among fools' that Richard Usborne calls him. Uncle George, with his 'frivolous young scallywag' (p.27) misses the mark, too. No one merely frivolous would take the Code of the Woosters so seriously. It enacts certain standards of sexual propriety – 'There is a line, and we Woosters know when to draw it … Not spines. Knees, yes. Spines, no' (p.33). Bertie has such a code of honour as limits the excesses of a naughty schoolboy. But he is *naughty* – when he plans practical jokes, when he flees from Aunt Agatha's wrath. He lacks due respect for elders and for authority, whether it is patriarchal, or auntly – or exercised over and through the English language, English literary tradition, and English values.

Jeeves, Wooster, class and Englishness

3.30 'England' exists in the Jeeves stories as three *terrains*:

(a) London's West End,

(b) London's suburbia, inhabited by 'the proletariat',

(c) 'the country'.

There are foreign excursions to New York and to fashionable French resorts. Hence the array of classes presented in them is as follows:

(a) (i) upper class – landed and moneyed, (ii) servant classes dependent on the foregoing,

(b) rich Americans,

(c) (i) persons involved in the entertainment industries – show girls, barmaids, and so on, (ii) artists and writers,

(d) proletarians: (i) urban – genteel or rough, (ii) rural – invariably rough, but in a 'traditional', rustic way.

Needless to say, this picture does not reflect the actual class structure of England in 1930. It excludes the North even more thoroughly than the Georgians did. Even southern manufacturing industry gets no look in.

3.31 What is striking about Bertie in relation to all the Wodehouse classes is that he is equally at ease – or more commonly ill at ease – with all of them. He is perfectly ready to mingle 'incognito' in a village pub. He detests 'suburban parlours' (p.32) but has clearly been in a number of them, and Rhoda Platt's aunt makes him squeamish, but she is 'a friendly soul'. His family despise or at best tolerate him, his Drones Club friends take advantage of his good nature. His sole true confidant, his only 'close friend', is his servant, Jeeves. And Jeeves, paradoxically, while fastidious about his master's dress and reputation, cares nothing, as 'Indian Summer of an Uncle' shows, for Aunt Agatha's 'ancient lineage', and is quite prepared to marry off Uncle George to suit Bertie's temporary convenience. Jeeves isn't essentially a snob. Nor, despite his sensitivity to social gradations, is Bertie.

3.32 You will recall our discovery that Bertie's language is highly unstable. It is Jeeves who utters, who represents, correct 'King's English'. But Jeeves cannot, any more than either aunt, fill the vacuum in the Wooster world where effective Authority ought to be. Hence it is no surprise to find that various aspects of the 'dominant', Stanley Baldwin image of England are treated, in these stories, with disrespect. For example: *'The Englishman is made for a time of crisis, and for a time of emergency'* (Baldwin, 1937, p.13). Well, Bertie is hardly a model Englishman by these standards. His nerve fails him in Maudie's parlour (pp.33–4). Jeeves – a model Englishman for Hilaire Belloc – emerges triumphant from the crises. But he clearly doesn't fit Baldwin's model of the Englishman who 'may not look ahead ... may not heed warnings ... may not prepare'. Jeeves is all calculation. Englishmen are not *supposed* to be 'brainy'. 'The English schoolboy, for his eternal salvation, is impervious to the receipt of learning' (Baldwin, 1937, p.13). Well, that applies to Bertie and his friends, but they are hardly the types to run a Great Empire.

3.33 It is crucial to realize that the main market for the Jeeves stories was the USA. Americans, we may safely generalize, were intrigued by English aristocrats. They liked (as they still like) to imagine England as a realm of quiet villages, stately homes and ancient customs. But they were also attuned to laugh at aristocratic Englishmen – idle and rather ridiculous creatures compared to their go-getting US contemporaries. And they didn't like English *snobbery*; this was a problem faced by British propagandists in 1940 as they tried to draw the USA into war against Hitler.

3.34 Hence the *unsnobbishness* of Jeeves and Wooster was surely crucial to their transatlantic appeal. The Jeeves stories, furthermore, are facetious about the England *imagined* by Americans, but do not offer any *alternative* England. They leave illusion comfortably intact. Wodehouse first became really successful in 1915, in the USA, and after the Second World War, dismayed by English reaction to his chatty broadcasts from Berlin to the American public, he went to live there permanently. Jeeves is as much a phenomenon of American popular culture as he is of British. It is surely significant that Uncle George's marriage to Maudie conformed to American anti-snobbery. And there are other instances in Wodehouse's fiction where aristocratic *English* marry non-titled *Americans*.

3.35   In George Orwell's view, Wodehouse's 'attitude towards the English social system is the same as his attitude towards the public-school moral code – a mild facetiousness covering an unthinking acceptance' (Orwell and Angus, 1968, p.397). But it is easy enough, I think, to explain why this implicit acceptance of a social system which we may now find strange and abhorrent doesn't interfere with our pleasure (if we experience it) when reading Wodehouse today. While he does not seriously *challenge* the system, he is constantly irreverent about the ideology of 'Englishness' which *supported* it. Indeed, the canon of English literature itself is subverted by Jeeves's and Bertie's quotations, which haul Golden Treasures of English Poetry into farcical contexts and give them ludicrous application.

3.36   In the next section, Graham Martin considers the poetry of W.H. Auden, another Englishman who was, eventually, to make his home in the USA. But Auden's perception of the country of his birth was, as we shall see, more disruptive and critical than the version Wodehouse constructed for export.

4   W.H. Auden

4.1   The aims of this section are:

(a)   to illustrate and consider the view of 'Englishness' emerging from Auden's poetry of the 1930s, using as an epigraph a line from *The Orators* (1932, p.62): 'What do you think about England, this country of ours where nobody is well?'

(b)   to contrast Auden's practice and conception of poetry with that of the Modernists discussed in Block 2 *The Impact of Modernism*.

4.2   W. H. Auden was born in York in 1907. A year later, his father moved to Birmingham, where he worked as School Medical Officer for the city. Auden was educated at private boarding schools, first in Surrey where he met Christopher Isherwood (b.1904), later to become a close friend, then at Gresham's School, Norfolk. From an early age, he was a voracious reader with wide intellectual interests, especially in mining engineering, the career that he first planned for himself, though he also started writing poetry when he was fifteen. In 1925, he went to Oxford University intending to study biology, considered switching to a degree in philosophy, politics and economics, finally settling for English literature and language. His reasons weren't at all academic. Having decided he would be a poet, he wanted an official excuse to read widely in English literature. In 1930 Faber published his first collection of poems, and others followed in 1932, 1936, 1937 and 1940, as well as several plays. Of these, *Look, Stranger!* (1936) earned Auden the King's Medal for Poetry. During the thirties he first worked as a schoolmaster, then briefly for the GPO Film Unit and, as his reputation grew, his publishers funded journeys to Iceland and China from which, in collaboration with Louis MacNeice (1907–63) and Christopher Isherwood, other books resulted. Following the outbreak of the Spanish Civil War in 1936, he visited Spain, where he did some broadcasting for the Republican Government. Early in 1939, he left England for New York, where he continued to live for the greater part of his life. He died in 1973. Politically, Auden was left-wing, and though not a member of the Communist Party during the thirties, he was sympathetic to its anti-capitalist, anti-imperialist and anti-fascist stance, especially in its direct relevance to 'the condition of England': the socio-economic crisis brought about by the Depression and the mounting political menace of fascism in continental Europe. At school, he came to realize that he was homosexual, and though this is not an explicit subject in his poetry, at a time when homosexual acts were accounted criminal, it seems reasonable to think it a powerful factor in his development as an 'outsider' and radical critic of English society.

'England ... where nobody is well'

4.3 The poems, essays, reviews and quasi-dramatic writings composed between 1927 and 1940 and assembled in *The English Auden* (edited by Edward Mendelson, 1977) fill 461 closely printed pages. So the poems printed in the Poetry Anthology amount to a tiny proportion of his output during the period. However, they represent the kind of poetry that earned Auden his high reputation and extensive influence during the decade.

ACTIVITY

Now please read through these poems, and listen to 'A Summer Night' and 'A Bride in the 30s' on Audio-cassette 2 Side 1. Then, make your own notes on the following issues:

(a) Several of the poems invoke 'love'. What idea or ideas of 'love' do they convey? Is 'love' always a *good thing*?

(b) The public world of contemporary history is often alluded to. What attitude towards it does the speaker of such poems convey?

(c) In a later poem, an elegy for W.B. Yeats, Auden states that 'poetry makes nothing happen' (Mendelson, 1977, p.242). Is this an accurate account of these poems? Do any of them attempt to make 'something happen' and, if so, what?

It's not essential on a first reading to grasp every detail of the 'meaning' of the poems. Some have allusions which may not be familiar, and you will find notes on these in the Poetry Anthology.

SAMPLE ANSWERS

(a) Auden uses the term 'love' in different ways. Sometimes, it means an impersonal energy which animates all living creatures, and which human beings inhibit or deny at their own peril. In this sense, 'love' means something like 'desire'. In contrast, there is also 'romantic love', whereby lovers retreat to a private world of illusory security in neurotic regression from adult life. Occasionally, there is also an idea of 'love' as a beneficent deity which can cure all human ills.

(b) The poems present contemporary history (the poverty caused by the Depression, the rise of European fascism, a perhaps imminent socialist revolution) as a threatening reality, indifferent or actually hostile to the personal happiness of the poems' speakers and of their friends/lovers, an objective state of affairs which demands immediate attention and (perhaps) participatory action.

(c) Some, though not all, of the poems appear to want 'something to happen', but such action is urged less upon the reader than upon the poem's speaker or friend. In general, most of the poems criticize a state of personal isolation and neurotic self-regard, and recommend a facing-up to the dangers of contemporary life.

If you didn't find it easy to sort out your first impressions of the poems – on a first reading, wholly understandable – browse through them again in the light of my generalizations, looking for evidence to support, or qualify, or contradict them.

ACTIVITY

We'll now consider some of the poems in more detail. Please re-read 'A Summer Night'. Its theme is the contrast and conflict between private happiness and public events. It's carefully constructed. Can you see how its structure reflects the conflict between the private and public spheres? Look also at the role of the scenes and images drawn from nature. How do they contribute to the poem's concluding resolution of the private/public conflict?

DISCUSSION

I hope you had no difficulty in seeing that the poem has three clear sections. The first five stanzas present the speaker's private world of security, happiness and mutual love. The next five stanzas move to the public world, not just England, but Europe, to the 'doubtful' political acts on which the security of the private world rests, and to the ignored, yet threatening claims of the poor, the hungry and the oppressed. The last six stanzas then invoke, through metaphor, impersonal forces which will destroy the speaker's private world, and then lead to a new dispensation in which private happiness, no longer in conflict with the public world, will 'to that strength belong'. We can perhaps summarize this sequence as *thesis* (the desirability of private happiness), negated by *anti-thesis* (the reality of public misery and oppression), the conflict between them resolved in a new *synthesis* (a transformed public world which harmoniously incorporates private happiness).

I suggested also that you look at the role of scenes and images drawn from nature. In the first section, nature is beneficent, kind to human desire: 'windless nights', 'the sexy airs of summer', a welcoming pastoral 'land of farms' and, psychologically, a healing presence. But in the second section, nature, as represented in the moon, is neutral, alien to the human scene, looking down without comment or preference on the speaker's friends in other parts of England; then from 'the European sky' bleakly noting the products of human culture (churches, power stations, picture galleries); and 'To gravity attentive' (notice the double meaning) seeing nothing of significance in the speaker's private world and ignoring the sentimental romanticism whereby lovers convert the moon into a symbol of 'the tyrannies of love'. This objective 'lunar' viewpoint allows the speaker to register the public world of oppressive and violent politics, of

> The gathering multitudes outside
> Whose glances hunger worsens;

without denying that *he* still remains within the safe and privileged world of those 'whom hunger *cannot* move'. (Why? Because privilege ensures that they don't go hungry.) And this double stance is crucial if the later synthesis of private and public worlds is to be plausibly imagined by this speaker.

The pun on 'gravity' has introduced the notion of impersonal forces, which the last section of the poem now develops, at first a little obscurely (stanzas 11 and 12), but then with more images from nature, not the congenial 'humanized' presence of the first section, but of its destructive/creative energies: a flood 'taller than a tree' bringing monsters from the ocean depths which will sweep away the speaker's privileged world. Then, after the cataclysm, when the flood subsides, nature's creative energies will finally combine with human agricultural skills to produce food, and with industrial techniques, to build new ships. This productive reconciliation of the human and the natural recurs in the last two stanzas. Personal love ('for which we [now] dread to lose /Our privacy') will *then* resemble the 'unlamenting song' of a child through whom sound 'the drowned voices of his parents', and will possess the calming therapeutic power of nature in the first section.

How convincing did you find this *synthesis* in which the poem concludes? What forces and impulses will bring it about? We shouldn't forget that it takes the form of an appeal, a hope, perhaps even a prayer ('*May* this...'). So should we press such questions? But see if you can formulate your ideas on this point, to which we'll return.

ACTIVITY

Please now re-read 'A Bride in the 30s'. What main points of similarity do you find between it and the poem we've been discussing? How, principally, does it differ?

SAMPLE ANSWER

(a) Some points of similarity: the contrast between private and public worlds; private relationships as a retreat from the threatening public world of police states; the association of 'luck' with fulfilled love ('Lucky, this point in time and space...'; 'Lucky to love the new pansy railway ... and in the policed unlucky city /Lucky his bed').

(b) Some points of difference: the link between 'love' and escapist illusion is more prominent, indeed, almost the whole subject of the poem.

> [Love] from these lands of terrifying mottoes
> Makes worlds as innocent as Beatrix Potter's;
> Through bankrupt countries where they mend the roads
> Along the endless plains his will is
> Intent as a collector to pursue
>   His greens and lilies.

Also, there are two kinds of 'love'. The quotation above refers to romantic escapism, and is nominated 'Love' with a capital letter. Later in the poem, we find 'love' as impersonal desire, which has no plans or 'opinions of its own'. Wholly obedient to individual human choice, it can take any form, any public expression, malign or beneficial:

> Crooked to move as a moneybug or a cancer
>   Or straight as a dove.

Which is to say, if suppressed or censored, its manifestations will be 'crooked', leading to such diseases as money-grubbing or cancer. And as well as the contrast between private and public worlds, there is a direct link.

> Be deaf too, standing uncertain now,
> A pine tree shadow across your brow,
> To what I hear and wish I did not:
> The voice of love saying lightly, brightly –
> 'Be Lubbe, Be Hitler, but be my good
>   Daily, nightly.'

Lovers can replicate the erotic relationship between dictators and the adoring masses they enslave (see stanza 6). The 'beautiful' beloved who enjoys the uncritical adoration of the lover corrupts both self and lover.

Lastly, the poem is more explicitly than 'A Summer Night' a direct appeal from the speaker to his beloved, both tender and desperate. The fate of their relationship depends upon the beloved making the right choice, resisting the temptation to be like Hitler, to exercise 'that power to excess /The beautiful quite naturally possess', to bask in the adoration of the lover whose own temptation, rooted in the neuroses built up during childhood, is to settle for self-destructive idealization of the beloved. Here, we can also notice a similarity with 'A Summer Night': the poem's speaker is both inside and outside the situation. He is its analyst, yet as the poem develops, reveals himself as equally capable of making the wrong choice.

ACTIVITY

Please now read 'Perhaps'. What idea of 'love' does it engage? Is this idea similar to the ideas of 'love' in the two previous poems? More generally, how far does this poem share their concerns?

SAMPLE ANSWER

Here 'Love' is invoked as a healing power associated with 'thoughtless Heaven' (that is, without thought, a spontaneous giving), a spiritual dimension suggested, perhaps, in 'A Summer Night', but not present in 'A Bride in the 30s'.

Nor does the theme overlap with 'A Bride in the 30s', but there are clear points of contact with 'A Summer Night', just as its structure is also tripartite. In the first four verses, 'Love' is urged to display its power over 'our little reef' to help us grasp, as did Newton, those impersonal laws (like the law of gravity) that link England with the rest of the world. The next seven verses chart the outcome of a long historical process concluding in the death of the bourgeois/entrepreneurial class which had carried through the English industrial revolution. The last four verses then envisage the possibility of violent future changes:

> ...prepared to lay on our talk and kindness
> Its military silence, its surgeon's idea of pain;

The link here with 'Our kindness to ten persons' in 'A Summer Night' is explicit.

Another similarity, less of theme than of the speaker's relation to the situation in the poem, lies in the use of the term 'our' throughout each section. On the one hand, the speaker is offering an impersonal analysis of the contemporary world, yet he doesn't exclude himself from it, nor from the effect of the possible revolutionary energy which

> Drives through the night and star-concealing dawn
> For the virgin roadsteads of our hearts an unwavering keel.

As with 'A Summer Night', what are your thoughts about this conclusion? How does it resemble or differ from the forecast of revolutionary transformation in the earlier poem?

BLOCK 3
'ENGLISHNESS'

ACTIVITY

Please now read 'The Malverns', turning where necessary to the notes on various details in the Poetry Anthology. In the poems we've discussed so far, the speaker has been, as it were, both inside and outside the situation he describes. Is this the case here? What is he saying about 'England'? What is his attitude towards it? And towards himself? One critic discerns a contradiction between the last stanza (where the speaker defines his position by means of two quotations) and the attitudes implied in stanzas 4 and 5. What might this contradiction be? Do you agree with the critic? And looking at the poem overall where do you think its strength lies – in the whole argument, or in the detail, or to some degree in both?

DISCUSSION

The poem is largely the speaker's debate with himself about his responsibilities towards 'the condition of England' as he now describes it. Primarily, he is the detached analyst, surveying the scene from a position of vantage, picking out key details, sketching a historical explanation, reporting the condemnatory voice of 'the thunder', and the self-condemnation of 'the bones of the war' (that is, those killed during the 1914–18 war). Though outside this state of affairs, the speaker is also self-critical. The opening three stanzas recollect an earlier occasion when, in the company of a lover, 'England to our meditations seemed /The perfect setting'. Their private happiness had allowed them to ignore the Depression when:

> Europe grew anxious about her health,
> Combines tottered, credits froze,
> And business shivered in a banker's winter
>   While we were kissing.

You'll have noticed, I hope, that this is a succinct version of the private/public contrast the other poems have dealt with. 'To-day no longer occupied like that', he looks carefully at the real world, hoping to know it better and be more involved in its problems. There is also emphatic self-criticism in the message of 'the thunder' which addresses the speaker as a member of a dying class ('Already behind you your last evening hastens up'). In contrast, 'the bones of the war' address him as 'cousin', recounting 'our' failures, which is to say, those of the previous generation. And the poem ends, not by assimilating the speaker to the death of his class, but in his affirmative decision to follow the teaching of two writers, Wilfred Owen and Katherine Mansfield.

> These moods give no permission to be idle,
> For men are changed by what they do;
> And through loss and anger the hands of the unlucky
>   Love one another.

Notice 'unlucky', and the different conception of 'love' it implies. This 'love' will not separate itself from 'the policed unlucky city' of 'A Bride in the 30s'.

An implicit contradiction between this and stanzas 4 and 5 was noted by Edward Mendelson (1981, p.241). The speaker wants to be 'rooted in life', yet in stanza 4 he merely looks at it (with even a touch of condescension?):

44

> A digit of the crowd, [he] would like to know
> Them better whom the shops and trams are full of,
> The little men and their mothers, not plain but
>   Dreadfully ugly.

While stanza 5, in explicitly analytic mode, dismisses all party-goers, romantic sentimentalists, cinema audiences, and the religiously devout as varieties of the entirely 'self-absorbed'. Mendelson's point is that such attitudes show little affection for the 'life' in which the speaker wants to be 'rooted'. What did you think about this? My answer would point to the last stanza's insistence that 'men are *changed* by what they *do*', which looks forward to a different state of mind from the one displayed in this poem. Nevertheless, Mendelson's points deserve attention.

As to the poem overall, considered as a self-examination, there are some real puzzles and even shadowy areas. Stanza 3 begins: 'For private reasons I must have the truth, remember /These years have seen a boom in sorrow'. What are these private reasons, and what truth? Not surely about the public state of affairs, which the verse sets out. So presumably private? Is this a hint at his reasons for breaking out of the escapist isolation of the love affair? The reader, I feel, is told either too little (if the subject *is* important, it shouldn't remain 'private'), or too much (as it stands, it distracts from the analysis of contemporary England). Again, the accusation which the 'thunder' aims at the speaker as a member of his class ('Has not *your* long affair with death /Of late become increasingly serious') isn't really answered. How has the speaker escaped from a general predicament that includes him? How can we be certain that he has?

Lastly, the poem stops, rather than concludes. The speaker returns from his point of analytical vantage to 'my situation' with what seems to be a promise of action. But what has his self-examination taught him that will help him to take action? And what sort of action? Despite the confident phrasing, too many questions go unanswered. So it seems to me that rather than the overall structure and argument it's the detail of the poem that makes it impressive – 'saxophones moaning for a comforter', 'empires stiff in their brocaded glory', to pick two at random – as well as the rhythmic mastery of the complex unrhymed eleven-lined stanza, which is an important poetic source of the poem's ambitious range and outward self-confidence.

ACTIVITY

Please now read 'Birthday Poem'. This, too, is a poem of self-examination, setting the speaker's past against the perceived crisis of the present. How, principally, does it differ from 'The Malverns'? Notice in this respect the dedication to Christopher Isherwood. How does the speaker convey his sense of the present, and what does he recommend for the future? Auden was later to omit this poem (with several others) from the American edition of *Collected Poems* (1945) because, one critic has suggested, it 'might have been thought excessively personal in its account of Auden and Isherwood' (Spears, 1963, p.154). Does the poem strike you as excessively personal?

DISCUSSION

One substantial difference is the absence of a general historical/psychological explanation for the contemporary state of affairs, which narrows the scope of the poem, but also disposes of the question raised and not answered in 'The Malverns', about the speaker's relationship to such a history. The poem is thus more 'personal', less about the class of which the speaker is both member and outsider than about changes in his own life. Another difference arises from the question: to whom is the poem addressed? 'The Malverns' is formally self-addressed, a kind of public soliloquy, yet also by implication addressed to the class whose death is said to be imminent, a doubling and ambiguity which amounts to its central difficulty. But in 'Birthday Poem' the addressee is explicit: a close friend who has shared with the speaker both an unsatisfactory juvenile past (stanzas 4–7), and a conviction that the present 'hour of crisis and dismay' demands new thinking and new action. So, as self-examination, the poem involves none of the puzzles and uncertainties of 'The Malverns' about why, now, the speaker takes a new view of public life. The poem tells us exactly why. Both speaker and friend are identified as writers, and the poem's focus is their public responsibility in that role. Their first efforts (stanzas 4 and 5) amounted to irresponsible adolescent pranks ('All the secrets we discovered were /Extraordinary and false'), a mere reaction against family and school, in effect, against the privileges of their class. Then followed (stanza 6) the period when 'love' was to be the all-encompassing solution of public calamities:

> Was there a dragon who had closed the works
> While the starved city fed it with the Jews?
> Then love would tame it with his trainer's look.

Both these stages are dismissed (stanza 7) as forms of private escapism. What the contemporary world (stanzas 8–10) really demands is a kind of writing that will 'Make action urgent and its nature clear' and whose insights will give the strength needed 'to resist /The expanding fear, the savaging disaster' (stanza 11). The last stanza returns us to the situation of the first, the speaker meditating on his immediate present, thinking of his friend, and remembering that both of them, as well as the holidaymakers he began by describing

> ...all sway forward on the dangerous flood
> Of history, that never sleeps or dies,
> And, held one moment, burns the hand.

A third difference lies in the way the contemporary world is presented in the allegorical mode of stanzas 9 and 10, where vices (Scandal, Falsehood, Mediocrity, and so on) triumph over the virtues (for example, Courage, Truth, Beauty). Instead of historical/psychological analyses about the death of his class, the speaker provides a blunt moralizing attack, though not without touches of appropriate contemporary detail. This treatment accords with the style of moral self-examination, the plea for 'pardon' for earlier inadequacies, and for the kind of writing the speaker praises in the 'strict and adult pen' of his friend which will reveal the seedy reality beneath 'the colours and the consolations' of contemporary culture. Isherwood, remember, was a novelist, and the poem may even be suggesting that the perils of the time cannot be responded to adequately in *poetry*, which in its turn may explain why, in envisaging the future, the conclusion offers no specific role for the speaker.

What did you decide about the perhaps 'excessively personal' character of the poem? I don't find it so, because it's not about a personal relationship between the speaker and his friend. It recounts a shared past in which they misused or misdirected their abilities as *writers* (the speaker perhaps more than the friend from whom in stanza 7 he begs pardon for his own failures). The sense of their personal friendship is strongly conveyed but always within the constraint of their identity as writers.

ACTIVITY

'What do you think about England, this country of ours where nobody is well?' This question is raised by a character in *The Orators* (1932), Auden's most substantial single work of the early thirties. Taking it as a leading clue, let us now draw together what the five poems we've been considering in some detail have to say about 'the condition of England'. What sickness do they point to? What is the cause, or causes, of this sickness? Do they suggest any cure, or cures? Can poetry contribute to the process of cure? How does the speaker of the poems (assuming now that the individual speakers closely resemble each other) conceive his relation to contemporary England? Is he going to do something about it or merely confine himself to saying his piece in these poems? Or perhaps a mixture of both?

Return to your notes on the poems and, where necessary, re-read the texts, before formulating your thoughts about the general issue.

SAMPLE ANSWERS

(a) England's sickness is illustrated by two kinds of symptom: social and psychological. Socially, there is the evidence of the industrial Depression, the failure of socially productive practices and institutions, the widespread illusion that England is a protected special case (unlike 'the sombre skies of Europe') and the conviction of a few (the speaker and his friends or lovers) of an approaching, and even welcome, violent change, product of a long and inescapable historical process. Psychologically, there is the unhealthy preference for isolation and loneliness, an inability to love (conceived as desire), or a misappropriation of love's impersonal energy on behalf of 'Love' as romantic escapism from social awareness and responsibility.

(b) The general cause of this state of affairs is 'historical', the imminent death of the dominant class, originally creators and leaders of the industrial revolution, and of the worldwide British empire, now sterile and afraid, half in love with the death that will soon overtake them.

(c) As to a cure, there is only the approaching historical catastrophe, the details and content of which remain vague, and – though the point is hardly explicit – the hope that the call to greater social responsibility and self-knowledge that the poems provide may be beneficial for those who read them. The last two poems suggest, if anything, that what is required is 'action' and not poems, but the terms of such action are unspecific, even obscure.

(d) The speaker's relationship to this state of affairs is complex, even ambiguous. In some poems, he is both the analyst and truth-speaker, almost a prophet crying 'the end is at hand', yet at the same time, himself infected by the condition being analysed. Only in 'Birthday Poem' is he sufficiently *not* part of the situation to make confident judgements about it, and these are more moralistic rather than historical. Yet even here, his future course is indeterminate, subject as he is, like everybody else, to 'the dangerous flood of history'. In general, we can say that the speaker *wants* to contribute to a better state of affairs, but (is it fair to conclude?) doesn't know how he can. The confident tone of the historical surveys, the range and specificity of detailed observation, the subtlety of diagnosis, repeatedly conclude in vagueness of prognostication and deeply uncertain feeling about how, in the future, to proceed.

ACTIVITY

Please now read 'Paysage Moralisé', a poem very unlike those we have discussed. How, primarily, does it differ? At the same time, do you see any connections between its subject and the general view of 'England' which the other poems convey?

BLOCK 3
'ENGLISHNESS'

SAMPLE ANSWERS

'Paysage Moralisé' includes no social, political or psychological detail. It is not a 'personal' poem. There is no mention of 'Love' or 'love', no self-examination, no historical survey, no evocation of imminent revolution. Formally speaking, it is more tightly organized than any of the previous poems, while its language is evocative and metaphorical. Valleys, mountains, islands, cities: each represents an aspect of a general human condition and the six stanzas play variations on their interrelationships.

Yet there are points of contact. From the earlier poems, we've seen that 'cities' represent a positive human aspiration however flawed in actuality. In 'Birthday Poem', the people escape from everyday working life to isolated 'islands' of pleasure and entertainment, just as an 'island' had been the location of the speaker's juvenile writings. And 'mountains'? In 'The Malverns', a mountain is the place for analysis and meditation from which the speaker has to descend to the uncertainties and challenges of living. The poem's conclusion provides the main clue for its overall direction:

> It is the sorrow; shall it melt? Ah, water
> Would gush, flush, green these mountains and these valleys,
> And we rebuild our cities, not dream of islands.

'Water', remember, had such a creative function in 'A Summer Night', as the symbol of the coming revolution, and in 'Birthday Poem', the process of history is a 'dangerous flood'. In 'Paysage Moralisé' that specific social-historical dimension is absent. The conclusion is less a prophecy than an appeal, even a despairing one. And notice that the appeal concerns 'the sorrow', a general human condition of endlessly frustrated hopes and misdirected aspirations symbolized in the previous stanzas: rotting harvests, starving cities, mountains climbed 'to get a view of islands', islands dreamt of as places of innocence and happiness, and valleys which 'moping villagers' refuse to leave.

Though 'Paysage Moralisé' has no explicit bearing upon 'the condition of England', I think these metaphorical links establish it as a companion piece to the other poems, conveying, in general terms, the same structure of feeling about the poet's contemporary world.

Auden and Modernism

4.4 Let us now turn to the second of the two aims of this section, the contrast between Auden's kind of poetry and that of the Modernists discussed in Block 2.

4.5 It will be useful here to sketch in the main influences on Auden's early work. When he began writing at school, Thomas Hardy (1840–1928), Edward Thomas (1878–1917), and Walter de la Mare (1873–1956) provided the first models, though unlike them, his preferred imaginary world was not rural, but one of industrial machines, usually derelict. As he was later to write: 'Clearer than Scafell Pike, my heart has stamped on /The view from Birmingham to Wolverhampton' (Mendelson, 1977, p.175). At Oxford, he first came across Anglo-Saxon poetry, the metrical schemes and rhetorical devices of which contrasted strikingly with the tradition of later English poetry, and soon affected his own. His discovery of T.S. Eliot's work led to a more radical change. He explained to his Oxford tutor that: 'to "understand" a poem was not a logical process, but a receiving, as a unity, a pattern of co-ordinated images that had sprung from a free association of sub-conscious ideas, private to himself' (March and Tambimuttu, 1948, p.82).

4.6 Eliot's poetry, evidently, was the channel through which Imagism, as an influence, reached Auden, but the mention of 'sub-conscious ideas, private to himself' indicates a different kind of influence: the psychology of Sigmund Freud. The work collected in an early volume, *Poems* (1930), illustrates the first point, as for example, these lines:

> You whom I gladly walk with, touch,
> Or wait for as one certain of good,
> We know it, we know that love
> Needs more than the admiring excitement of union,
> More than the abrupt self-confident farewell,
> The heel on the finishing blade of grass,
> The self-confidence of the falling root,
> Needs death, death of the grain, our death,
> Death of the old gang; would leave them
> In sullen valley where is made no friend,
> The old gang to be forgotten in the spring,
> The hard bitch and the riding master,
> Stiff underground; deep in clear lake
> The lolling bridegroom, beautiful, there.
>
> (Mendelson, 1977, p.40)

The images are vivid and economical (lines 6, 12–14), and also, if not exactly private, laconic and withheld (lines 13–14). But you'll also have noticed another style (lines 1–4, 8–11), discursive and abstract rather than imagistic, which we can trace to the poet's direct preoccupation with ideas, giving much of his poetry a bookish, intellectual character, strikingly unlike that of the Modernists for whom ideas could only be conveyed indirectly through imagery, covert allusions, or brief quotations.

4.7 Yet another model – the poet as teacher – was provided by Wilfred Owen (1893–1918). Owen had drafted a preface for a volume of his work which became widely admired during the thirties, and these sentences from it show why:

> Above all I am not concerned with Poetry.
> My subject is War, and the pity of War.
> The Poetry is in the pity.
> Yet these elegies are to this generation in no sense consolatory. They may be to the next. All a poet can do today is warn. That is why true Poets must be truthful.
>
> (Owen, 1931, pp.40–1)

4.8 As we've seen, Auden quoted 'the poetry is in the pity' in 'The Malverns'. But the last two sentences are more relevant to the way he conceived his own task: the need to warn, and equally to be truthful. This meant a rejection of the Modernists' insistent separation between poetry and 'a message', between art and the world of moral, political or social action. His *Poems* (1930) contains several poems in the Modernist manner, striving for a self-sustaining artistic unity and linguistic autonomy. His more characteristic thirties poetry refers directly to the world that is *not* poetry, to the mounting social and political crises which the poems we've looked at try to confront.

4.9 Auden's poetry during the thirties shows, then, a dual impulse. On the one hand, the times were out of joint. They demanded that the poet utter imperative warnings and necessary truths, even at the risk of preaching or lecturing. On the other hand, a poem that is nothing *but* preaching or lecturing is in dire trouble, and Auden knew this as well as anybody. What was his solution? How did he reconcile these conflicting demands?

BLOCK 3
'ENGLISHNESS'

ACTIVITY

Please now read the extract in the Reader (pp.178–80) from Auden's preface to an anthology, *The Poet's Tongue* (1935), which he co-edited. What main point does it make that seems to you relevant to the problem Auden was struggling with in the poems we've looked at?

SAMPLE ANSWER

I would pick out his rebuttal of the 'propagandist, whether moral or political', who insists that the writer should devote his powers to persuading people to undertake some action. Auden insists, to the contrary, that:

> ...poetry is not concerned with telling people what to do, but with extending our knowledge of good and evil, perhaps making the necessity for action more urgent and its nature more clear, but only leading us to the point where it is possible for us to make a rational and moral choice.
> (pp.179–80)

Like the Modernists (see Block 2 paragraph 8.5) Auden rejects the notion that poetry should preach or lecture, but unlike them he claims that there is an explicit connection between poetry and 'action'. Poems can clarify and deepen our grasp of the problems we face, thus 'making the necessity for action more urgent and its nature more clear'. I hope you noticed that this phrase occurs, almost word for word, in 'Birthday Poem'.

DISCUSSION

How does this conception of poetry relate to those poems we have discussed? It seems to me to explain their primarily analytic approach to their subject, 'the condition of England', the social, economic and political situation confronting Auden in the thirties. The poet's task is to understand these problems as fully as possible, setting them in their historical context (as in 'The Malverns' and 'Perhaps'), identifying the various forms of escape from the moral challenge of the time by means of 'love' or neurosis ('A Bride in the 30s'), and analysing his own predicament ('A Summer Night', 'Birthday Poem'). The extract also includes Auden's reply to 'the psychologist [who] maintains that poetry is a neurotic symptom, an attempt to compensate by phantasy for a failure to meet reality' (p.179). This alludes to a Freudian conception of art as essentially escapist, to which Auden's reply is that while subconscious elements richly contribute to the creative process, this process also requires much hard and entirely conscious work. In an essay about the significance of Freudian ideas from the artist's point of view, he wrote:

> even in a short lyric, let alone a sustained work, the material immediately 'given' to consciousness, the automatic element, is very small ... what [the writer] is most aware of are technical problems, the management of consonants and vowels, the counterpointing of scenes...
> (Mendelson, 1977, pp.336–7)

If you think back to the elaborate formal pattern of 'Paysage Moralisé', or 'A Summer's Night', or 'Birthday Poem', you will find ample evidence of such poetic *work*.

Nevertheless, Auden accepts that much art is 'escapist', and this represents another way in which he differs from the Modernists, 'high seriousness' being an essential feature of their writing. In the essay about Freudian ideas, he wrote:

> There must always be two kinds of art, escape-art, for man needs escape as he needs food and deep sleep, and parable-art, that art which shall teach man to unlearn hatred and learn love...
>
> (pp.341–2)

And he defined parable-art in this way:

> You cannot tell people what to do, you can only tell them parables; and that is what art really is, particular stories of particular people and experiences, from which each according to his immediate and peculiar needs may draw his own conclusions.
>
> (p.341)

I'll leave you to consider which of the poems we have looked at most nearly represents 'parable-art'. For my view, you can turn to page 55, but not before you have formulated your own.

ACTIVITY

Lastly, we need to look at the kind of 'poetic language' illustrated in Auden's work. Please first re-read from Block 2 Section 6, 'Poetic language', the pages discussing Valéry's ideas (paragraph 6.32). How does Auden's poetic practice accord with such ideas?

SAMPLE ANSWER

Checking through the list of points I noted at the beginning of paragraph 6.32 in Block 2 which summarize Valéry's position, Auden's poetry tends to the *prosaic* (points (a) and (e)). It more resembles 'walking' than 'dancing' (point (b)). Of the poems we've considered, only 'Paysage Moralisé' corresponds to the Valéry notion of poetry, though even here, in the last three lines which call for the 'rebuilding of cities', the poem declares a non-poetic function.

DISCUSSION

You will remember, though, that Valéry's view of poetic language, widely influential on all Modernist writing, was a sign and a symptom of a social and cultural crisis in which writers and readers had become mutually estranged. Auden mentions this in his 'Letter to Lord Byron' (1936), where he surveys the main changes in poetry and art since Byron's death, and describes this alienation of writer from reader as thoroughly undesirable. He contrasts it with the healthier state of affairs during the eighteenth century, when:

> Each poet knew for whom he had to write,
> Because their life was still the same as his.
> As long as art remains a parasite
> On any class of persons it's alright;
> The only thing it must be is attendant,
> The only thing it mustn't, independent.
>
> (in Mendelson, 1977, p.186)

Here, evidently, is one clue to his own poetry as he strives to recover for it the 'character of communicative speech' (Block 2 paragraph 6.32) which Symbolist poetry had lost. Auden wants a poetry that *isn't* 'independent', that

BLOCK 3
'ENGLISHNESS'

has readers in view who share, or at least sympathize with, Auden's assumptions and values; to whom, and therefore also on behalf of whom, his poems can speak. His poems, far from aiming to be self-sustaining and autonomous verbal structures, directly address themselves to non-verbal events and contexts, which is to say, to the social and political condition of contemporary Europe which threatened the poet, just as much as his readers. To put the contrast sharply, when Eliot writes:

> Under the brown fog of a winter dawn,
> A crowd flowed over London Bridge, so many,
> I had not thought death had undone so many.
> Sighs, short and infrequent, were exhaled,
> And each man fixed his eyes before his feet.
>
> (*The Waste Land*, I, lines 61–5)

both scene and crowd are details within a special Eliotic vision of the world, a modern Inferno. When Auden writes:

> August for the people and their favourite islands.
> ...Lulled by the light they live their dreams of freedom;
> May climb the old road twisting to the moors,
> Play leap-frog, enter cafés, wear
> The tigerish blazer and the dove-like shoe.

though we notice the symbolic reverberation of 'islands', neither scene nor people are overwhelmed by its implications, but persist with a life of their own.

But does this mean that Auden's poems show none of the characteristics described in Jakobson's account of the 'poetic function' of language which Modernist poetry exhibits in high degree? In Jakobson's analysis the 'poetic function' dominates over the others when 'the principle of equivalence' is more strongly present than 'the principle of combination'. We saw that a key effect of this kind of writing is to make the reader more aware of the words as *words*. In such examples as 'I like Ike', 'In for a penny, in for a pound', the aural 'equivalences' dominate over the 'combinative' sequence. Thus, to take the first example, we do not read it as a statement about a personal relationship (on the model of 'she likes John') between 'I' as subject and 'Ike' as object of the verb 'like', but rather as a new composite word which joins speaker, political commitment, and political goal in a complex unity. How far, then, does Auden's practice fit such an account of the 'poetic function' of language? Can we say of particular stanzas or poems that 'the principle of equivalence' is dominant? Consider these two stanzas:

> They built by rivers and at night the water
> Running past windows comforted their sorrow;
> Each in his little bed conceived of islands
> Where every day was dancing in the valleys,
> And all the year trees blossomed on the mountains,
> Where love was innocent, being far from cities.
>
> But dawn came back and they were still in cities;
> No marvellous creature rose up from the water,
> There was still gold and silver in the mountains,
> And hunger was a more immediate sorrow;
> Although to moping villagers in valleys
> Some waving pilgrims were describing islands.

Where can 'equivalence' be found here? First, rhythmically: each line is only a slight variant on the familiar five-stress pattern, each stanza has six such lines, each end word is a disyllable, stressed on the first of the pair, and more subtly, the same six end-words recur in each stanza, the main difference being that 'water' ends the first line of the first stanza, and 'cities' the first line of the second. The effect binds the two stanzas together so that though time passes between the first and the second, as if in some narrative sequence, the rhythmic equivalences work against this, reinforcing the point that nothing has changed, that 'they' are trapped in the same unhappy condition, still in unsatisfactory 'cities', still dreaming of 'islands', instead of rebuilding the 'cities'.

And we can see 'equivalence' at work at the semantic level. The whole poem is constructed round the pattern of the end-words, six stanzas, each of six lines, with the same end-words, so that the sixth line of the sixth stanza ends in 'valleys', which concluded the first line in the first stanza. You'll remember, I hope, the discussion of rhyme as a form of 'equivalence' where we noted that the aural similarity of rhyme words seems to imply semantic similarity (Block 2 Section 6). In Auden's poem the end-words are not rhymes, but the rhythmical similarity and the cycle of repetitions provide a rhyming effect, which in its turn suggests a semantic link. And this is entirely germane to the poem as a whole because, as we've seen, the six concepts (valleys, water, sorrow, mountains, islands, cities) mutually define each other. The structure of the poem sets them within a network of interrelationships which belong only to this poem, and which modifies, if it doesn't actually displace, their ordinary referential meaning.

In discussing Geoffrey Hill's 'September Song' (Block 2 Section 6), we saw that the 'poetic function' loosened the ordinary relationship between word and referent, creating uncertainties and instabilities of meaning especially appropriate to a poem confronting the horrors of Belsen and Auschwitz. As a general clue to the effect of 'poetic language', this is worth following. Auden's poem demonstrates such an effect in its own way.

ACTIVITY

But 'Paysage Moralisé' is very unlike the other Auden poems we have looked at. Does the 'principle of equivalence' also apply to them? What about the opening stanzas of 'Birthday Poem'?

Look at the rhythmic patterning of each stanza. Does it resemble that of 'Paysage Moralisé'? Are there rhymes? Is there a rhyming effect? Does 'the principle of equivalence' show its presence in other ways? The terms 'islands', 'valleys', 'city', and by implication 'water' (first stanza, line eight) all appear. How do they resemble/differ from their role in 'Paysage Moralisé'?

SAMPLE ANSWERS

(a) The basic rhythm of each line is five-stress, but the variants are more striking and there are many run-over lines, as for example:

> The efFUSive WELcome of the PIER, and SOON
> The luxURiant LIFE of the STEEP STONE VALleys.

This makes a striking contrast with 'Paysage Moralisé', where the five-stress pattern is held to much more closely, and there are no run-on lines.

(b) There are no rhymes. The end-words don't have the repetitive pattern of 'Paysage Moralisé'. So no rhyming effect.

(c) Nevertheless, 'equivalence' shows in the fact that each stanza has eight lines, a pattern held to by the rest of the poem, and by and large despite the run-on lines, each stanza builds up by way of single lines, each contributing a distinct item. Moreover, within single lines, the aural patterns show 'equivalence' at work with its internally binding effect. Did you notice the alliteration and assonantal echoes in:

> The luxuriant life of the steep stone valleys
> ...
> Are caught by waiting coaches
> ...
> Lulled by the light they live their dreams of freedom

and the rhythmic repetition in:

> The tigerish blazer and the dove-like shoe.

The effects here are less complex than in 'Paysage Moralisé'. We can say that they mark off the sentences as belonging to 'a poem' without contributing in any more specific way.

(d) 'Islands', 'valleys', 'city' and 'water' differ from their role in 'Paysage Moralisé'. Partly, they are items in a described scene. That, surely, is the reader's first impression? Yet closer attention reveals that the suggestion of detailed 'reference' is countered by its opposite. The people live in 'stone valleys' in 'the city' (that is, close-packed terrace housing running up the streets of industrial cities), and have temporarily escaped to holidays in *favourite* islands' – not particular islands which the verse then depicts but locations for their 'dreams of freedom'. These 'islands' are the range of pleasures mentioned in the next verse, as well as actual islands with piers and arriving steamers full of holiday-makers. The terms thus look both ways, towards 'reference', but also towards a 'poetic' function peculiar to the stanza.

DISCUSSION

If we now consider this kind of writing in relation to the whole poem, we can say that the contrast with 'Paysage Moralisé' reflects Auden's need to address contemporary problems which 'make action urgent', demanding that the writer should take up a position, and present a point of view, while holding to the conception of poetry illustrated in the prose extracts, that it is not the job of the poet to urge upon his readers a particular course of action – moral, social or political. 'Birthday Poem' is built upon what Jakobson calls a 'combinative sequence', an argument and a narrative that concludes in the lines about 'the dangerous flood of history', and its language shows a 'referential function' in certain details of the stanzas we've looked at, and of later ones, about the past that the writer and his friend have shared. But as a poem of self-examination, it also turns back on itself, ending where it began with the writer looking out 'From the narrow window of my fourth-floor room ... [watching] reflections /Stretch in the harbour', and its language also reveals 'the poetic function' in other details, stanza by stanza. We can understand the rhythmic contrast with 'Paysage Moralisé' in the same terms. The absence of rhymes and the run-on lines have the effect of presenting a speaker, and as a poem addressed to a friend, this is very necessary. 'Paysage Moralisé', in contrast, adopts an anonymous and impersonal voice, and its patterned rhythms and tight structure move it away from any suggestion of direct speech, except perhaps in the last three lines.

4.10 For a concluding exercise, you could now work through one or other of the poems we have already discussed, to see whether their general resemblance to 'Birthday Poem' is revealed also in details of language.

4.11 On page 51, I asked you to consider which of the poems discussed could be considered as 'parables', and how far they exemplified Auden's general view about poetry. 'Paysage Moralisé' is surely 'a parable' and in the sense of not telling the reader how to act, all the poems accord with Auden's general 'aesthetic'. Two shorter poems in the Poetry Anthology which I haven't discussed, 'Now the leaves are falling fast' and 'O what is that sound', are also parable poems.

5 *Consciousness in fiction*

5.1 This section will build on earlier discussions of other aspects of narrative and provide you with an analytical tool you will find useful generally, and particularly when you come to read the opening sections of one of the major texts in the block, *England Made Me*.

5.2 In Block 1 Graham Martin discussed the nature of prose fiction as one of the three types of text that make up the bulk of texts in this course. The word fiction comes from the Latin *fingere*, meaning to fashion or shape. The writer creates an imaginary world peopled by characters whose actions and personalities are mostly invented and represented by language. Dennis Walder's concern in Block 2 Section 3 was to make you aware of how narrative operates to create different chronological effects as an aspect of structure.

5.3 On Audio-cassette 1 Side 2 he introduced you to the idea of 'narrator' and 'focalizer' – 'who speaks' and 'who sees'. The 'focalizer', you will recall, is the narrative agent who provides the voice and/or perspective. In this section, I want to take this a little further in terms of how 'consciousness' is presented in narrative.

5.4 Perhaps the fact that consciousness *is* presented in fiction is so obvious that we tend to take it for granted. When we read a story, for example, 'Indian Summer of an Uncle', we *expect* to know what is going on in Bertie's mind, besides what he actually says and does. Yet, if you think about it for a moment, this intimacy may be the really distinguishing factor about this type of fiction and perhaps what has made it so popular. In drama our knowledge of the inward lives of characters is restricted to what they tell us about it, either in conversation or in the form of soliloquy. (I shall leave poetry aside here because it does not depend on a number of characters to function in the same way as most fiction and drama.) Of course, both conversation (or 'dialogue') and self-declaration ('monologue') are found in fiction too, but in more varied and subtle ways than simple utterance.

5.5 The narrator (not to be confused with the author) is responsible for the organization of the discourse in the fiction and has access to the innermost thoughts and feelings of the characters portrayed, even to those they might hardly be aware of. It is this power that makes fiction so intimate and powerful a form. As the novel has developed over the centuries, critics have attempted, in various ways, to analyse and differentiate between the manners in which authors have used this power. As in most kinds of analysis, a basic language has developed to use as a tool. You have already come across one example of this in Block 2 Section 3 where, in narrative, Chatman makes the distinction between *histoire* (story) and *discours* (discourse).

5.6 One of Genette's contributions to our present subject, consciousness in fiction, was to distinguish between pure narration (which he calls 'diagesis' 'statement of the case') and a presentation of life through dialogue (which he calls 'mimesis' – 'imitation of words and action'). (He took these terms from Plato.) Another way of putting it is

diagesis = telling, or 'story'

mimesis = showing

5.7 Between these two poles is what is known as 'free indirect speech' (*style indirect libre* in French, *erlebte rede* in German) which you have already come across in Audio-cassette 2. Here is another example of 'free indirect speech', though the use of 'sponged' is actually 'reported speech':

> He believed quite sincerely that he had never 'sponged'. He had borrowed, of course; his debts to relatives must by now have almost reached the thousand mark; but they remained debts not gifts, one day, when a scheme of his succeeded, to be repaid.
> (*England Made Me*, p.10)

It is 'free' because it is not actually vocalized in a precise place at a particular time, 'indirect' for the same reason (there is no 'he said'), and 'speech' because it uses the words in sentences that Anthony Farrant would use to express his thoughts.

5.8 Another way of describing this manner of presenting Anthony Farrant's consciousness would be to call it 'narrated monologue' – the monologue is what he is thinking, but it is mediated through the narrator. 'Narrated monologue' is one of three terms coined by the American critic Dorrit Cohn, whose work I shall be using as a basic 'language' for thinking about how consciousness is presented in fiction. Of course, there are other 'languages' which could be used for this purpose, for there are no fixed 'rules' about how a text is discussed. As Cohn points out in her book *Transparent Minds*, all the means of analysis I have mentioned so far assume that consciousness/thought is always *verbal* (which in novels it is, of course). This is still a contentious issue, and some critics/psychologists argue that all thought must, ultimately, be in a language of some kind. Nevertheless, most people would agree that not all *experience* is verbal, and experience is part of consciousness. To overcome this difficulty, Cohn has coined a new term, 'psycho-narration', which she describes as identifying 'both the subject-matter and the activity it denotes (on the analogy to psychology, psychoanalysis)' (1978, p.11).

5.9 Cohn's third term (the first two being 'narrated monologue' and 'psycho-narration') is 'quoted monologue', or representing a character's thoughts directly, unmediated by the narrator. She sums up each of these in this way:

> 1 psycho-narration – the narrator's discourse about a character's consciousness
>
> 2 quoted monologue – a character's mental discourse
>
> 3 narrated monologue – a character's mental discourse in the guise of the narrator's discourse.
> (Cohn, 1978, p.14)

The distinctions between these are perhaps more easily seen in the example she gives of how one perception can be presented in different ways:

> 1 psycho-narration
> He wondered if he was late.
>
> 2 quoted monologue
> (He thought) Am I late?

3   narrated monologue
    Was he late?

She sees these techniques of presentation as corresponding to different *levels* of consciousness, ranging from what psychologists call the 'unconscious mind' to the fully conscious. So, in this scheme the psycho-narration technique corresponds to the edge of the unconscious (which includes the non-verbal), while 'quoted monologue' presents the contents of a conscious mind direct and unmediated.

5.10   Of these techniques, 'psycho-narration', though the most common and so taken for granted, is probably the least well-known and therefore deserves closer attention. Expanding on her initial explanation, Cohn distinguishes between 'dissonant' and 'consonant' forms. In 'dissonant narration' the narrator is prominent and 'even as he focuses intently on an individual psyche, remains emphatically distanced from the consciousness he narrates'. 'Consonant psycho-narration', on the other hand, is 'mediated by a narrator who remains effaced and who readily fuses with the consciousness he narrates' (Cohn, 1978, p.26).

ACTIVITY

In *Mrs Dalloway* Virginia Woolf, in ridding herself of the 'scaffolding' of nineteenth-century novelists, makes much use of 'narrated monologue' and 'quoted monologue' and comparatively little of 'psycho-narration' in order to present the thoughts of her characters with as little interference from the narrator as possible, though the distinctions are not always easy to make. This is because, as Dennis Walder noted on Audio-cassette 1 Side 2, the narrative 'hovers' between narrator and character, and the narrator 'glides' in and out of the character. Take the opening pages of the novel: in the second paragraph on page 5, beginning 'What a lark! What a plunge!', we are given Clarissa's feelings and thoughts in both past and present. How does this fit into Cohn's categories?

DISCUSSION

Well, the *words* are undoubtedly Clarissa's, though not spoken but mediated through the narrator. Is this not, then, 'quoted monologue' – 'a character's mental discourse'? Then a little further down the page we get an instance of 'narrated monologue': 'A charming woman, Scrope Purvis thought her (knowing her as one does know people who live next door to one in Westminster)'.

It is *narrated monologue* because, in conveying Scrope Purvis's view of Clarissa, the narrator incorporates the words he is using to express his thoughts on seeing her. As for true *psycho-narration*, it is not easy to find many examples, though the first entry of Septimus Warren Smith on page 21 provides one: 'So, thought Septimus, looking up, they are signalling to me. Not indeed in actual words; that is, he could not read the language yet...'.

It is significant, I think, that Septimus is insane and one of the few characters we do not get 'inside' in the novel, and so Virginia Woolf employs the less intimate method of conveying his thoughts. Finally, what *kind* of psycho-narration is this? In Cohn's terms, it is surely 'dissonant': the narrator is at a distance.

ACTIVITY

Would you now look back at 'Odour of Chrysanthemums', which you read in Block 1, and look for more examples of Cohn's three categories, particularly

5 CONSCIOUSNESS IN FICTION

later in the story after the possibility of the accidental death has been conveyed to Elizabeth Bates?

DISCUSSION

In fact, Lawrence employs mostly narrative, dialogue and psycho-narration to move through the events and emotions that make up the story. Cohn's other two categories are mostly absent, though there is an example of quoted monologue when Elizabeth hears the winding-engine:

> Again she felt the painful sweep of her blood, and she put her hand to her side, saying aloud, 'Good gracious! – it's only the nine o'clock deputy going down,' rebuking herself.
>
> (Prose Anthology, p.74)

The paragraph beginning 'Elizabeth's thoughts were busy elsewhere. If he was killed…' provides an interesting example of psycho-narration. We know it's a paragraph about her conscious mind from the mention of 'thoughts'. Then, we also know that the words are not Elizabeth's but the narrator's because they are not cast in dialect. What kind of psycho-narration is this? I think it is of the 'consonant' kind because the narrator is close to Elizabeth's mind.

'Odour of Chrysanthemums' also illustrates a sub-verbal kind of psycho-narration where words are not involved in conveying consciousness. When we first encounter Elizabeth Bates we are left in no doubt as to her state of mind, though no thoughts as such are involved:

> For a few moments she stood steadily watching the miners as they passed along the railway: then she turned towards the brook-course. Her face was calm and set, her mouth was closed with disillusionment.
>
> (p.65)

Her state of mind is expressed in her facial expression and, since the narrator is keeping at a distance, it is sub-verbal psycho-narration of a *'dissonant'* kind.

5.11 So far, I have been considering texts all set in the *third-person narrative*. When we read a *first-person narrative*, like the Bertie Wooster stories, the situation is clearly different, for the narrator, not the author, is the sole mediator of all that happens: *everything* is seen through his eyes, in Woosterian fashion. (On the other hand, this doesn't mean that the narrative that results is simply fictional autobiography: autobiography is usually in the first person but the converse is not true.) Will the three categories discussed so far in relation to third-person narrative hold good for first-person narrative? The answer is 'yes, to some extent', though, as Cohn points out:

> …analogues between third- and first-person narration should not obscure the obvious and crucial differences between them: even when a narrator becomes a 'different person' from the self he describes in his story, his two selves remain yoked by the first person pronoun.
>
> (Cohn, 1978, p.144)

ACTIVITY

One such analogy is applying the categories 'dissonant' and 'consonant' to self-narration: autobiography is clearly of the 'consonant' kind. What about the Wooster stories? How would these categories work there?

DISCUSSION

Only, I think, in terms of Bertie's *consonant self-narration* since all is seen through his recall. As he is not noted for being a deep thinker, and his narratives in these stories are full of actions rather than reflection, there is no self-quoted or self-narrated monologue. Instead, there is a great deal of dialogue, sometimes for pages at a time so that the effect of a drama is gradually built up. (Waugh, who admired Wodehouse greatly, used the same technique in his fictional writing.)

5.12 What are the pros and cons of this style of presentation in terms of 'presentation of consciousness in fiction'? Taking the Wooster stories as our example we gain a powerful, distinctive impression of Bertie since the story is principally narrated through his language, employing his neologized verbs and slang. This does not, however, exclude his reproduction of Jeeves's voice, which, by the conventions of fiction, we allow him to bring in. If we did not allow this, then the narrative would become monotonal and this is obviously a potential drawback of first-person presentation. The real limitation from an author's viewpoint (if he or she has chosen to work within a certain vein of realism) is that the narrative can get into the mind of a character only to the extent of the narrator's knowledge of him/her.

5.13 Most of the fictional prose in this course, however, is written in the third-person mode of presentation and so we shall be returning to the techniques associated with that type of writing in the next section.

5.14 You will find Greene's narrative technique in *England Made Me* rather more experimental than in his later work and (as I suggested at the beginning of this section) the 'tools' for analysis you have acquired in this section should prove useful in untangling how he achieves his effects.

6 Graham Greene: 'England Made Me'

6.1 In Section 1 we looked at the different ways in which versions of Englishness could be constructed, focusing in particular on the importance of the English male public school. W.H. Auden, whose work Graham Martin discussed in Section 4, was a product of this British institution. In a different way, so is Anthony Farrant, one of the principal characters in *England Made Me*, though Greene's interest in the question of national identity goes beyond the legacy of school. Greene has always been a great traveller and has chosen to live most of his adult life on foreign soil as an expatriate, so perhaps he is well qualified to look at England 'from the outside'.

6.2 Many of you will have read other novels by Greene, perhaps some more explicitly Catholic in theme than *England Made Me*. Radio 4 *Home and Abroad* examines this aspect of Greene's writing in some detail, but in our chosen text it is of tangential interest, mostly in relation to Minty's beliefs. Nevertheless, *England Made Me* is a novel with serious themes and judgements of both individuals and institutions. It is one of Greene's earlier works, and yet it has stayed constantly in print over the last twenty years as its intrinsic interest in

BLOCK 3 'ENGLISHNESS'

terms of both theme and technique has been increasingly recognized. Greene began writing the novel in November 1933. It is set in Sweden, which Greene visited specifically to gather background, as he later recalled in an introduction to the novel: 'I think it is the only occasion when I have deliberately chosen an unknown country as a background and then visited it, like a camera-team, to take the necessary stills' (1970b, p.vii).

6.3   He had a particular reason for choosing Sweden, as we shall see later. You may have read the novel already: whether or not this is the case, initially I want to read the opening pages of the novel with you. It is structured in seven parts, each subdivided into sections.

ACTIVITY

Please now read the first two parts (that is, up to p.66), making notes on the following questions as you do so:

(a)   What might the title mean?

(b)   What is the significance of the epigraph by Walt Disney?

(c)   How do Parts I and II indicate the novel's main subjects?

(d)   Bearing in mind the earlier discussion on the presentation of consciousness in fiction and the discussion of narrative in Block 1, summarize Greene's technique in these opening sections.

DISCUSSION

(a)   The eagle-eyed may have spotted on the imprint page that the novel has two titles – in England it was called *England Made Me* but in the United States it was published as *The Shipwrecked*, perhaps because the English title would have been off-putting to potential American readers. Each title is revealing in its own way. *The Shipwrecked* clearly means 'shipwrecked people', so drawing on the powerful metaphor of the Ship of Life and suggesting a destiny of failure and disaster. *England Made Me*, on the other hand, has a curious ring. Is it ironic? Or defiant? Or comic? I think it is all of these. Greene chose to set his novel outside the British Isles. In doing so, by distancing the location from England, he at once secures a quite different perspective on his characters, most of whom are in fact English. But who is the 'me' of the title? It may refer not to one specific character but several – Minty, Anthony, Kate, the Minister. And what was the process of 'making' – social mores, education, culture? I shall come back to these questions.

(b)   'All the world owes me a living.' This cryptic sentence must, I think, be meant mainly for Anthony, and it epitomizes his childish egocentricity and emotional backwardness, his refusal to face reality. In a wider sense it could be taken to represent a more general sense of self-centredness: Krogh's concern for Krogh, Minty's for Minty, and so on. (It certainly applies to Krogh's ruthless manipulation of other people's money.)

(c)   The first three sections (forming Part I) are all devoted to Kate and her twin brother Anthony. The first sentence gives an immediate indication of the uneasy nature of their relationship: 'She might have been waiting for her lover' (p.7).

This suggestion is taken up again when his landlady at the lodgings assumes the same, whispering that they will 'not be disturbed'. Greene explores with some subtlety the personalities of the brother and sister and their complex relationship in the opening section, for this (he said later) was the novel's major theme. The other major subject of the novel, the ethics of international finance, is introduced in Part II which begins with Krogh in his office awaiting Kate's return from England. His attitude to his business is made clear in two short sentences: 'Success: he was quite certain he deserved it ... honesty was a word which never troubled him' (p.35). When news of a strike arrives and socialism is mentioned (p.48), a political edge to the novel begins to emerge. Greene was to comment in later years:

I think of those years between 1933 and 1937 as the middle years for my generation, clouded by the depression in England, which cast a shadow on this book, and by the rise of Hitler. It was impossible in those days not to be committed.

(Greene, 1970b, p.vii)

The interviews in TV5 *Left and Write* illustrate the truth of his final observation.

(d) Greene employs a mixture of methods, beginning in the first section with what was defined earlier as 'psycho-narration', in this case in the third person, that is, the novel is not narrated by one of the characters but by another party. Most of the first section is seen through Kate's thoughts and feelings whereas Anthony is presented straight, though some of his long-held views are brought into the account. This is what Cohn calls the 'consonant' type of narration: the author is not distancing himself from Kate but closely identifying his narration with her presence in the scene.

The second section of Part I modulates into a different style and pace of narrative. It takes a moment or so to grasp that all the events recalled are relayed through Anthony's thoughts and memories, and so Greene has switched here to first-person narration, which gives a powerful impression of Anthony's life to date. It is a technique that produces a cumulative, kaleidoscopic effect. You might be tempted to call it 'stream of consciousness', though it isn't quite that because it ranges backwards in time, representing past incidents like running away from school which involve minimal snatches of dialogue. Its great virtue is that we are given a searching account of the way Anthony's mind works which, because he is shallow and unreflecting, would have been difficult to convey in any other way. It is not altogether easy to follow on the first reading of the novel, for incidents are related the full significance of which only becomes clear in the light of later events.

In the third section of Part I, the author reverts to 'psycho-narration' of the 'consonant' kind – most of the events are seen from Kate's point of view. In places, Greene also uses 'quoted monologue' and straightforward third-person description to show what is going on in Kate's mind. Look at pages 24 and 29:

The thought came to her: If I could put back time, if I could twist this ring Krogh gave me and abolish all this place...

She recognised at once that the moment had passed. He was as far away from her as ever he had been in the Shanghai Club, on the Aden golf-course. It had been less self-knowledge than a temporary break in the cloud of his self-deception.

In both cases the reader is given Kate's actual thoughts, in the first instance in words she would have used though mediated through the narrative discourse. The second example is straightforward third-person narration.

BLOCK 3
'ENGLISHNESS'

Part II begins with an initial portrait of Krogh. Greene eventually felt he had failed to bring Krogh to life as a character, but it was not for want of trying and one of the means he uses is, in our adopted language, 'dissonant psycho-narration' – the narrator in no way empathizes with the character and conveys Krogh's thought processes in language Krogh would not have used: 'Again he was obscurely troubled by the idea that he had neglected something. The statue in the court came back to worry him' (p.36).

Towards the end of this first section there is an example of 'quoted monologue': 'A man in my position ought to have protection, he told himself, but police protection had to be paid for in questions...' (p.40). Somehow this fails to be convincing: is it perhaps that the actual words don't really seem to be Krogh's in the way that Anthony's are Anthony's? And is this perhaps related to the fact that we know Anthony is English and Krogh is not, yet the thoughts of both are mediated through the English language?

England Made Me, a novel of action (even with a 'thriller' element), is also much about the inner lives of its characters considering either their immediate thoughts or their deeper natures. Take the third section of Part II (p.59) where Anthony meets Minty and, afterwards, reflects on his situation: 'This place, he thought, will do as well as another; it's better than Shanghai; I can get along with Minty and earn enough...'. Here we are given Anthony's thoughts in a flow which is perhaps best called 'narrated monologue': it comes close to 'stream of consciousness' but does not have the random quality associated with that style of writing.

There is a wide range of experimentation in technique in this novel. When Greene comes to Kate in the fourth section of Part II, he switches to first-person narration and, in what is really a monologue (though it contains recalled conversations in which others speak), she presents her own mind and past events to the reader. In terms of our adopted language, it is 'self-narration' of a dissonant kind – the narrator is distanced from the past she recalls. The first sentence ('I wake and Erik sleeping and his cold hand on my side', p.62) indicates that Kate is in bed so the effect Greene seeks (and achieves) is, presumably, her thoughts in a state of consciousness verging on sleep, hovering between conscious and unconscious.

6.4 Please now read right through to the end of the novel, bearing in mind the two main themes identified by question (c) above, and that the theme we are pursuing in Block 3 is 'Englishness'.

6.5 I want to continue discussion of *England Made Me* by considering its subject, characters and themes under several different headings. Let's start with the relationship between Kate and her twin brother Anthony.

Anthony and Kate

6.6 Here is how Greene saw his novel, looking back thirty-five years later in 1970:

> The subject ... was simple and unpolitical, a brother and sister in the confusion of incestuous love. I found it odd to read once in a monthly review an article on my early novels in which a critic *disinterred* this theme ... There was no ambiguity in *my* mind; the ambiguity was in the minds of Kate and Anthony whom I had chosen for my 'points of view'. They were continually on the edge of self-discovery, but some self-protective instinct

warned them off, with false or incomplete memories and irrelevancies, the moment of discovery. Kate was nearer to knowledge than Anthony and both used their superficial sexual loves, Kate with Krogh and Anthony with Loo, to evade the real right thing. The cowardly evasions were not mine: they belonged to the doomed pair.

(Greene, 1970b, pp.x–xi)

6 GRAHAM GREENE: 'ENGLAND MADE ME'

6.7 Was it obvious to you that the relationship between Kate and Anthony is 'incestuous'? 'Doomed' they certainly are, and there is a disturbing, uneasy quality to their relationship. According to Greene's biographer, Norman Sherry, the title he originally used in his diary for the book was *Brother and Sister*, and yet the very first sentence shows Kate as if 'waiting for her lover', hastily repairing her make-up, knocking back gin on her own in a station bar. It isn't until the second page that we learn it is her brother she is waiting for. Greene's skill in depicting their complex and unhappy relationship lies precisely in suggesting, through a number of small details, rather than simply stating, that theirs is more than a simple sibling friendship. For one thing, there seems to be a reversal of gender-related qualities: '…she was his elder by half an hour; she had, she sometimes thought with a sense of shame, by so little outstripped him in the pursuit of the more masculine virtues, reliability, efficiency, and left him with what would have served most women better, his charm' (p.9).

6.8 Then, meeting him at lunchtime in Sweden, it is Kate, again, who orders the drinks, only to earn her brother's disapproval: '"You do put it down, Kate," Anthony said, signalling to the waiter … He disapproved, he didn't believe in girls drinking…' (p.25). As this passage indicates, Kate is dominant in the relationship: it is she who has the contact in Krogh and who tries to persuade Anthony to accompany her. At his lodgings there is a strong hint of jealousy as Kate, looking at a photograph of one of Anthony's women, asks 'Is this her scent on the pillow?' She then experiences tremendous relief as he finally agrees to go with her: '"What a pair we are." She could have sung with joy, when he pulled her to her feet, because they were a pair again…' (p.15).

6.9 As the novel unfolds, the hopeless nature of Kate's love for her brother emerges in small but significant ways: meeting him with the Davidges, and overhearing their conversation 'She listened with jealousy, affection…' (p.21). Anthony later accuses her of being jealous of Loo and at one point, though ostensibly referring to Kate being too late for lunch, they come to the brink of an admission: '"Tony," Kate said, "if you weren't my brother –" She let the sentence drift away over the crumbs and the soiled glasses unfinished, meaningless. What was the good? "You'd be gone on me," Anthony said, turning on her the same glance as he turned, she knew, on every waitress…' (p.24).

6.10 There are several moments of this kind: another comes as the pair are awaiting Krogh's arrival. Krogh will give Anthony a job not because Kate loves her employer but because she loves her brother (p.53). Then when the sexual side of Kate's relationship with Krogh and Anthony's with Maud is mentioned, the scene erupts into violence, he hitting out at the wardrobe, she attempting to strike him. As Anthony reflects on the incident later, calling it 'love', the displaced nature of these liaisons, which Greene calls 'evasions', becomes clear: 'But love, he thought, that means me and Maud, you and Krogh. "That is my bedroom," she had said when he pointed at a door and a little later she had tried to strike him with her fist' (p.61).

6.11 Kate's passion for her brother is real: 'She watched him with an undisguised devotion that startled him, a devotion of the blood, not of the brain' (p.78). There is one point where Anthony comes close to a realization of his feelings, but the moment passes, to be lost forever:

BLOCK 3
'ENGLISHNESS'

> The inadequate words fumbled at his heart. She says what she means, she knows what she wants, she does what she likes, a fellow can trust her. He wanted to tell her that he loved her, but a light went on above a door, and she said: 'That's Erik. He's ready for you.' The opportunity had gone…
>
> (p.79)

6.12   Kate, on the other hand, is still making her humiliating attempts to hold on to her brother right up to their final meeting on the night that he is killed:

> But already she had begun to plan how they might be together again. She knew she might have prayed; the temptation was there, to fall back on eternity, on other people's God, the emotional cry in the dumb breast, the nudity of confession: I love him more than anything in the world…
>
> (pp.194–5)

But Anthony has already decided to go to Loo Davidge because he is 'in love with her', and Kate dismisses him with 'Oh, go to hell'. Anthony's murder immediately after this brings the troubled relationship to an end: at the funeral we are given no hint of her feelings and learn only that, like her brother, she is 'moving on', to a new job away from Krogh.

6.13   In his retrospective Introduction which I quoted earlier Greene accuses these two characters of 'cowardly evasions' of the 'real right thing', which implies that he thinks the honest conclusion to their relationship would have been to admit their mutual need, though where the novel would have gone from there is another question.

ACTIVITY

Bearing in mind my earlier point about qualities associated with gender and the general theme of Englishness, how would you describe the characterization of Anthony and Kate respectively? Do you find them convincing?

DISCUSSION

Anthony cuts a pretty poor figure on almost every count: he is consistently deceitful, shallow and untrustworthy, while believing himself to be an English gentleman (that is, another definition of 'Englishness') except when it's convenient not to, as when he is seducing Loo. As such, he believes himself superior to Krogh: on their first meeting Anthony quickly perceives that he is 'only a poor bloody foreigner after all' (p.55). As an Englishman, he speaks no foreign languages, as he tells Minty, without any hint of apology, when spoken to in Swedish: '"I'm English," Anthony said. "I don't understand a word"' (p.56).

Greene later admitted that Anthony Farrant was 'an idealised portrait of my eldest brother Herbert' (1980, p.31), though quite what 'idealised' means here if not simply 'novelised' is another matter: I think it must mean that Anthony had *some* redeeming feature which Greene failed to find in his brother, whom he once described as 'an utter bounder'. Behind those three words lies a whole background of public-school mores and social practice which, the novel implies, is what theoretically Anthony should live up to and does not. (The dictionary defines 'bounder' as 'a would-be stylish person kept at or beyond the bounds of society', that is, someone who breaks the rules.) Nevertheless, the narrator's account of Anthony is, in Cohn's terms, 'dissonant' from the beginning. Meeting Kate, Anthony immediately displays 'automatic charm' and 'his humorous, friendly shifty eyes raked her like the headlamps of a second-hand car which had been painted and polished to deceive' (p.9). He is both 'dishonest' yet not 'dishonest enough', for he retains a childlike quality in believing his own lies. It is this curious combination that is to prove his undoing: on discovering Krogh's intended fraud, his first reaction is that it's 'not respectable', his second that it presents an ideal opportunity for blackmail ('He must make it worth our while, Kate', p.143). It is this knowledge that leads Hall to murder him.

Dishonesty is Anthony's overriding feature for, as Kate observes to herself, he 'can't open his mouth without lying', whether to her, the Davidges or himself. This dishonesty results in a curiously hypocritical code of ethics, never better exemplified than in his set of double-standards for men and women:

> He disapproved, he didn't believe in girls drinking, he was full of the conventions of a generation older than himself. Of course one drank oneself, one fornicated, but one didn't lie with a friend's sister, and 'decent' girls were never squiffy. The two great standards, one for the men, another for the women, were the gate-posts of his brain.
>
> (p.25)

Yet Anthony is also seen as a victim, for his shabby morality has been learned from 'the majors whom he had known lay down the moral law before smoking-room fires' (p.25)

> Anthony learning (the beating in the nursery, the tears before the boarding school) to keep a stiff upper lip, Anthony learning (the beating in the study when he brought home the smutty book with the pretty pictures) that you must honour other men's sisters. Anthony learning to love with moderation. Anthony in Aden, Anthony in Shanghai...
>
> (pp.63–4)

Anthony, although unlike Septimus Warren Smith in *Mrs Dalloway* in most ways, is like him in that he does not conform to the ideal of the English male acceptable to a culture dominated by middle-class values of 'proportion', decency and respectability.

His schooldays played a major part in this formation and his link with them is maintained in the wearing of an old school-tie, though not always that of his own school. He 'promotes' himself by wearing a Harrow tie, though he fails to deceive Minty for a moment. In fact, all the English male characters except Anthony and Hall are old Harrovians. His school days, we learn, contained a traumatic incident resulting in Anthony's running away until persuaded to return by Kate. This, it is suggested, was the first of his many attempts to 'escape', always ending in a 'resignation'. Yet Anthony hankers after a form of Englishness which, ironically, is produced by expatriatism. Like school, it is closely associated with snobbishness, class distinction and, strangely, maleness. In his first days in Sweden, Anthony sits in a café, feeling for his identity in a strange land using words from Rupert Brooke's celebrated poem quoted in Section 7 (see page 80), though the choice is more probably Greene's than his character's:

> If he wanted to ask for a match, to ask the way, he would not be able to make himself understood. The waiter brought his beer; it seemed to establish between them the elements of companionship because the man had understood at least that much. The pale lamps burning in the daylight dusk, the waiter who had served him, his chair, his table, 'some corner of a foreign field that is for ever England', he dwelt on them with a lush sad sentiment. His manner momentarily had a touch of nobility, of an exile's dignity...
>
> (p.74)

> The trouble, in a way, was that they were waiters; if they had been waitresses, it would have been so much easier to establish his English corner. Although he had travelled half-way round the world in the last ten

BLOCK 3
'ENGLISHNESS'

years he had never been far away from England. He had always worked in places where others had established the English corner before he came: even in the brothels of the East English was spoken.

(p.75)

Yet Anthony, whose only skill seems to be shooting at stalls in fairgrounds, has a freedom which Krogh envies and, for one evening at least, is able to share at Tivoli.

Greene's success with Anthony is that he makes convincing (and interesting) a character who, for the most part, is also made to look despicable. The authenticity of the character may lie not simply in its likeness to Herbert Greene but also to the rather surprising admission by the author that he had 'shared many of his experiences' (1970b). He seems to mean by this the frustrations and half-satisfactions of Anthony's sexual adventures.

Kate is surely one of Greene's saddest, most complex female characters. We are told nothing about her appearance and know only that she is thirty-three years old because that is her brother's age. She emerges as a figure both strong and yet vulnerable: she is fond of alcohol, as we learn from the first pages of the novel, and she later finds some amusement in guiding Anthony 'through the intricacies of the licensing laws' (p.30). She is also ambitious, freely admitting to 'using' Krogh 'from the start' (p.139). She continues to do so and to make sure that she and Anthony receive a good 'settlement' from their blackmail. Yet she has a sense of humour as her joke about the 'Order of the Celestial Peacock Second Class' (p.22) shows, though it is beyond the Davidges' comprehension. She is also, we learn, sterile and has no desire for children, as she tells Anthony when the question of marriage to Krogh comes up, to prevent her giving evidence against him at a trial in a court of law. The following passage makes this clear. How does it add to what we already know of the brother and sister?

> He [Anthony] was worried; he was muddled; he said something under his breath about 'children' and blushed with self-consciousness.
>
> Kate said: 'I'm sterile. You needn't be afraid', and seeing his embarrassment, added with an enraged despair: 'I don't want them. I've never wanted them,' and felt her body stretch to receive him. 'You're so conventional, Anthony', and she thought: a child inside me would be no closer than we've been, and yet there he stands, and there it would stand, blushing, self-conscious, my God, how prim, forgetting what they don't want to remember.
>
> (pp.143–4)

This passage clearly states her incestuous desire for her brother and it can be no coincidence that she tells Anthony he 'needn't be afraid' immediately after revealing her sterility. There is also here further evidence of the gender reversal I mentioned earlier: it is Anthony the male who thinks of childbearing and families, traditionally the woman's role which Kate rejects out of hand. This is evidence for the argument Dinah Birch presented in Block 2, that gender is socially constructed rather than biological; part of their relationship developed over the years since birth is that they seem to have adopted each other's roles.

For the most part, Kate is defined by her relationship with men, whether brother, employer or father. We learn something of her history in passing: she began training as a nurse, was found unsuitable and so went into office work for a firm owned by a friend of her father who then obtained the job with Krogh for her when his business failed. We learn that Kate's relationship with her father was not good: she disliked him, she remembers, because in spite of possessing good, essentially 'English' qualities, he was lacking in love: 'But these were his maxims. Do not show your feelings. Do not love immoderately.

Be chaste, prudent, pay your debts ... He read Shakespeare and Scott and Dickens and did acrostics all the days of his life. A little bit of England ... Why did I dislike him so?' (p.63).

His exact and cautious nature is summed up in his choice of wording for his wife's tombstone. The options are 'devoted' or 'affectionate' and he goes for the latter: '"affectionate husband", he did not grudge five letters in the good cause of accuracy' (p.63).

Kate also disliked him for the way in which he had ruined Anthony, teaching him false values, instilling lessons by beatings. There is also the fact that he would deeply have disapproved of her liaison with Krogh, her employer: one of his maxims had been 'A girl should not be seen at a play with her employer', let alone be lying in bed with him.

Yet in spite of her independence and strength, seen in her stratagems to save Anthony from the wrath of his father (p.137), Kate is also a tragic, vulnerable figure. When we first meet her, we are told that she feels 'tears of loneliness at her despairing, hopeless love for her brother'. How does she react to his death? This we are not told in terms of her feelings, though the final pages of the novel hint that she simply shuts out the experience: 'I'm simply moving on. Like Anthony' (p.207).

Another aspect of Kate, which is relevant to this block's theme of Englishness, is her deliberate attempt to deny national identity, in itself perhaps an ironic reflection on someone 'made' by England at this time. This is made clear early in the novel in response to Anthony's blimpishness:

> 'Listen,' she said. 'I can't leave you here without money. You're coming with me. Erik will give you a job.'
>
> 'I can't speak the language. And anyhow,' he leant forward on his stick and smiled with as much negligence as if he had a thousand pounds in the bank, 'I don't like foreigners.'
>
> 'My darling,' she said with irritation, 'you're out of date. There are no foreigners in a business like Krogh's; we're internationalists there, we haven't a country...'
>
> (p.11)

In what sense can England be said to have 'made' Kate? Just as London is important to Anthony (see p.138), so is a form of immoral internationalism with which she has deliberately chosen to surround herself:

> Deliberately she turned away from the thought that there had been a straightness about the poor national past which the international present did without. It hadn't been very grand, but in their class at any rate there had been gentleness and kindness once.
>
> (p.136)

> Her dusty righteous antecedents pulled at her heart, but with all her intellect she claimed alliance with the present, this crooked day, this inhumanity...
>
> (pp.138–9)

This 'international' quality is something Kate shares with the blonde 'high-class prostitute', the latter being 'gleamingly international' (p.172) and, though they see it as a virtue, my own feeling is that Greene is using it in a spirit of deep irony. There is another point that you might ponder: is Kate's lack of Englishness associated with the fact that she is a woman?

6 GRAHAM GREENE: 'ENGLAND MADE ME'

BLOCK 3
'ENGLISHNESS'

ACTIVITY

Kate remains an enigmatic figure in spite of the fact that she and her conscious mind (as we have seen) are at the heart of the book, as Greene intended them to be. Is she, however, the character most readers remember most vividly? Perhaps not, for in Part III of the novel Minty enters the scene. What is Greene's purpose in creating this character? Sum up your impressions of Minty and jot them down.

DISCUSSION

Minty is certainly an unusual, not to say eccentric, figure, who eventually cut across Greene's original plans for his novel. Greene later reflected, somewhat wryly:

> Anthony and Kate were the heart of the book; Krogh was only there to manipulate their story, and the others, Loo, Hall, Hammarsten, were background figures; no one else was needed. Then suddenly the boat listed because Minty stepped on board.
>
> (1970b, p.x)

His original purpose in creating Minty had been to act as a foil to Anthony:

> I suppose, for the purposes of Anthony's story, I had required as a minor figure, some fellow outsider who would recognise – as only a fellow country-man can – the fraudulent element in Anthony, who could detect the old Harrovian tie and know at once that it did not belong.
>
> (p.x)

Minty's very name is odd and sounds like a brand of sweet. He is an unprepossessing sight at his first entrance – 'small, wrinkled, dusty ... cocky and ingratiating' (pp.56–7) and the first hint of his oddness comes when he mentions popping 'across the bridge for a bite and Benediction', from which one might conclude that he is a Catholic (Benediction is a short service involving the reserved Blessed Sacrament). What is odd about this is the conjunction of the two, seeming to put having a snack on the same level as worshipping Christ's presence in the Host. When we meet Minty properly in Part III it turns out that he is 'a good Anglo-Catholic', though as the novel develops it becomes increasingly apparent that the adjective is used not without irony. (Greene was later to call him a 'sly pathetic Anglo-Catholic, a humble follower, perhaps, of Sir John Betjeman', 1970b, Introduction). Minty's religion is important to him: he has a Madonna on his mantelpiece, has invented his own expletive to avoid smut – 'Holy Cnut', that is, Canute. He says his prayers and attributes his recovery to health in a previous year on an August day to the intercession of St Zephyrinus, an obscure saint with the feast day of 26 August in the Roman Calendar, rather than that of the better known St Louis whose adjacent feast day is 25 August. Knowledgeable about the saints, Minty identifies with the 'despised, forgotton Zephyrinus', as later in his night prayers he fervently recites the Magnificat asking 'that God would cast down the mighty from their seats and exalt the humble and meek'. Yet Minty's feelings about his religion (if not his theology) are heretical for, in his disgust with anything to do with the human body, he cannot bear to think of Christ's incarnation:

> To think that God Himself had become a man. Minty could not enter a church without the thought, which sickened him, which was more to him than the agony in the garden, the despair upon the cross.
>
> (p.86)

ACTIVITY

Why do you think Greene appears critical and dismissive of Minty's religion?

DISCUSSION

Remembering Greene's own conversion to Roman Catholicism (discussed in Radio 4 *Home and Abroad*), I think it might be because it seems to be a kind of compromise which allows Minty to draw on the reassurances of religion yet which also allows him to behave with malice. This is the point of the passage about the two saints:

> Tomorrow he would have to remember to keep his mind free from malice and uncharitableness in honour of St Zephyrinus; today he could give full rein to every instinct.
>
> (p.84)

Minty can choose when to be good, when to dispel the malice that 'stirred in his veins, moved with the blood stream' (p.72). We can see this grotesquely illustrated by his behaviour with the spider when he decides to play God, controlling life and death, asking for mercy yet displaying cruelty. In fact, in the course of 'his day', which occupies the whole of Part III of the novel, we are given a detailed account of Minty, his family background, his absurd rituals with coffee and cigarettes and, significantly, for the purposes of this block, his sense of identity and nationality. It is not without irony that we are told about this:

> Presenting a dog-eared card at the Poste Restante counter he believed that, as an Englishman and an Old Harrovian, he honoured Stockholm by choosing it as his home. For no one could deny that he was a gentleman of leisure who might have lived in any place with a post office and scope for personality.
>
> (p.78)

The single adjective 'dog-eared' says it all: shabby, friendless, scraping a living, Minty retains his sense of superiority to others in general and foreigners in particular because of his background and public-school education. And yet in spite of his absurdity Minty actually does personify a certain kind of Englishness in his attachment to his school and his eccentric form of Anglo-Catholicism. Anthony sees this clearly on first meeting him:

> Anthony looked back and England was again outside, keeping a watch on him through the iron patterning of the gateway, one bloodshot eye on each side of a tender branching iron plant.
>
> (p.77)

Anthony is sitting in a cafe, thinking of home and deciding to return there, when Minty turns up. To Anthony he represents the very Englishness he is nostalgic for:

> ...he smiled and forgot his resolution because he saw England staring back at him through the glass with coat-collar turned up and dripping hat.
>
> 'Minty', he called, 'Minty', to the surprise of the waiters.
>
> (p.75)

But Minty is not altogether to blame for his behaviour for he is, like Anthony, a victim, a damaged person clinging on to life (remember the American title, *The Shipwrecked*?). Minty's particular hell was his experience at public school – Harrow – which is seen as Englishness epitomized. Minty has a peculiar love–hate relationship with 'the old place', as he calls it, even an obsession:

6 GRAHAM GREENE: 'ENGLAND MADE ME'

BLOCK 3
'ENGLISHNESS'

Ex for All, thought Minty. The school phrases stung his lips, but they were always first to his tongue. It gave him a bitter tormented pleasure to say, not an afternoon free, but Ex for All. He hated and he loved. The school and he were joined by a painful reluctant coition, a passionless coition that leaves everything to regret, nothing to love, everything to hate, but cannot destroy the idea: we are one body.

(p.83)

ACTIVITY

What is the significance of the particular metaphors employed in this passage?

DISCUSSION

The principal metaphor is sexual, 'a passionless coition', and so suggests a relationship that is a physical joining yet one entirely without joy. The final sentence, describing the school community as 'one body', is, of course, St Paul's description of the Christian Church whose members make up the 'body of Christ'. Yet, a little later, we are to learn how repulsive he finds the human body. To complete this complex account of his feeling towards the school and all it stands for, we are told that Minty was 'taken away by his mother' after 'long hours with the housemaster' for what, it is implied by mention of a 'chemist in Charing Cross Road', was some kind of sexual misdemeanour. This reference is picked up in the final chapter where Minty, recalling the only four friends he has had in life, thinks of

> Baxter who let him down when it came to the point, who would have nothing to do with the package of assorted goods from the Charing Cross chemist.
> (p.202)

Heaven is a place where there is 'no sex' and so when Anthony visits him with Loo looking for a place to have privacy, it comes as no surprise to learn that Minty

> didn't like girls, he couldn't have said it in words more plainly; tawdry little creatures, other people's sisters, their hats blocking the view at Lord's.
> (p.126)

Yet, although redolent of failure and reduced to letting his room out for a seduction, Minty maintains that most English quality, class consciousness, as he surveys the ridiculous Loo Davidge:

> He followed Loo with his eyes, maliciously observing every unfortunate point in her appearance. 'It was good of you to come.' But in his scorched eyes he expressed quite clearly the disapproval of the bad make-up, the cheap pretentious dress, the saucy hat. There were people these days one could not avoid meeting: but one retained standards.
> (p.127)

In the same vein, we know without being told that Loo's parents, with their carefully gauged gentility, are 'lower middle class'.

Earlier in the novel, Kate has reflected on Anthony's choice of girlfriends in similar class terms:

> She remembered Annette, and Maud swelling in a frame too small for her, the cheap scent on the pillow: he's always liked them common.
> (p.22)

ACTIVITY

One way and another, sex and sexuality feature quite largely in the novel. How are they presented, and are they related in some way to 'Englishness'?

DISCUSSION

On the whole, the question seems somewhat problematical. There is Anthony who is a philanderer, evading his attraction to his sister by collecting sexual conquests whose only value is to satisfy his vanity:

> it was vanity only which he experienced in the final act, it had never been anything else but vanity. One liked to make them helpless, to cry out...
> (p.129)

Then there is Loo herself, alternately risible and pathetic, who resents being called a virgin and boasts of her sexual experience, agreeing to go to bed with Anthony in a pert quotation from *David Copperfield* 'Barkis is willing' (p.120), and claiming that sexual activity is 'healthy'. Kate and Minty are, to say the least, unconventional in their sexual feelings. Even a minor character, Gullie, is caught ogling photographs of nudes under the pretence of interest in the human figure.

No explicit relation is made between the sexual behaviour of these characters and their nationality. On the other hand, the brief mention that is made of the Swedes' behaviour as observed by young Andersson and in Krogh seems entirely conventional, so there may be yet another irony to be taken from the novel's title in the practices of the English.

Krogh

6.14 I'd like now to turn to Krogh who, with the Anderssons and other Swedes, stands in contrast to the English characters. Greene based the character on a figure from real life who is mentioned on page 36 of the novel: 'Kreuger, lying shot in the Paris hotel, was his example'.

6.15 This reference would have needed no explanation to a reader in 1935, but it probably does now. In 1933 Greene had reviewed a biography of Kreuger who was, explains Norman Sherry, a manufacturer of matches who

> juggled with astronomical figures, lending large sums to governments in exchange for monopolistic concession ... his forgeries, discovered after his suicide, were like everything else he did, massive.
> (Sherry, 1989, p.484)

ACTIVITY

Yet, in spite of using a real-life model, Greene did not feel in later years that Krogh had really come to life as a character and conceded that he was 'only there for the sake of the story' (1970b, p.ix). Is this somewhat dismissive remark a fair assessment of Krogh?

DISCUSSION

If Krogh does not 'come to life', it is not for want of trying on Greene's part. We first meet him in Part II of the novel where his importance and standing are emphasized by the monogrammed buildings which form his offices. Perhaps Greene relies a little too much on this method of building him up, for

6 GRAHAM GREENE: 'ENGLAND MADE ME'

he never displays the stature which he is said to have and requires for the purposes of the plot. We learn early on that he is a crook: 'Honesty was a word which never troubled him' (p.55). He is also an atheist and a philistine, who has to rely on others to tell him whether a work of art has any value or not:

> 'I don't understand poetry,' he said reluctantly. He did not like to admit that there was anything he did not understand; he preferred to wait until he had overheard an expert's opinion which he might adopt as his own.
> (p.41)

Lacking the human touch, he has to remind himself to make a joke when visiting Andersson by writing the word 'joke' down and underlining it. We learn quite a lot about his past in Chicago and Barcelona and how he has come to his present success, but our interest is only really kindled when he is with other characters – Anthony, Kate, Hall. (It is an inherent problem in creating dull characters that they frequently become dull to read about.) Anthony, in particular, is able to bring Krogh out, largely through his patronizing self-confidence in his own opinions and actions which contrast sharply with his employer's anxious uncertainty about how others see him. But Krogh remains an insubstantial figure, even in his relationship with Kate, about which we are told very little. This seems to me a weakness in the novel, because the fraudulent activities which form the storyline all centre on his actions and so it is natural to expect a clearer picture, a stronger sense of the man. Bearing this in mind, I would like now to turn to what Greene saw as his secondary subject.

The economic background

6.16 Looking back on his novel of 1935, Greene later saw its subjects in these terms:

> The subject – apart from the economic background of the thirties and that sense of capitalism staggering from crisis to crisis – was simple and unpolitical, a brother and sister in the confusion of incestuous love.
> (Greene, 1970b, p.x)

Remembering that for a reader in 1935 the economic background would have been contemporary, it is conceivable that it would have been seen simply as a backdrop. But I wonder if that is how it strikes a later generation of post-war readers who have witnessed the rise of fascism, the Second World War, the spread and later collapse of communism, and then a later depression – not to speak of stock-market crashes and 'insider dealing' charges in the late 1980s. Perhaps what was 'background' to Greene came to assume a larger significance than he intended. It certainly seems as if that is how the novel was read by Paul Hogarth, the artist who illustrated the recent Penguin edition: underneath the title are just two men, one clearly Krogh in the foreground being watched by the other, presumably Anthony. There is no sight of Kate at all. It is, perhaps, slightly ironic that Krogh should dominate the cover, for he is one of the few main characters who has *not* been 'made' by England.

ACTIVITY

Yet if the fraud theme does assume a larger significance for a later generation of readers than Greene thought it might, how does it integrate with the other concerns? How satisfactory do you find this aspect of the novel?

DISCUSSION

I would argue that it is an appropriate 'backdrop' to the picture of rootlessness, dishonesty and doom in the personal relationships depicted in the novel. There is not one relationship of any importance that is portrayed as giving happiness and fulfilment. (It could be, of course, that Greene is deliberately portraying a fallen world, that this portrayal of greed and dishonesty reflects his belief in original sin, though nowhere is he as theologically explicit as that. But this novel is as good an example of 'Greeneland', that characteristically drab setting, as any among his work.) In Radio 4 *Home and Abroad*, I state that Greene's politics have always been on the 'left' rather than the 'right', in so far as those terms can be said to have meaning by themselves. In *England Made Me* it is Andersson senior, the strike organizer, who appears to have the narrator's approval, so it seems safe to assume that Greene is no advocate of the politics of greed. Then, when Kate describes Krogh's business on the last page in terms of a common phrase at the time ('We're all thieves'), Minty accuses her of socialism, which she denies. The politics are there, but although this novel was conceived and written during the 1930s when Greene seems to have found it as necessary to be committed as any of the people interviewed in TV5 *Left and Write*, there is no open political statement in *England Made Me*. Some readers may view this as something lacking in the book: the problem is described, and no solution or vision offered. Greene answered such a charge in an interview given in 1979 when he stated:

> A political commitment has never served as motivation for a book of mine. I don't believe that political action is part of a writer's function. In my view he is no more than an observer and I don't think I've gone outside the framework of my functions.
>
> (Allain, 1984, p.116)

The most vicious side of capitalist exploitation is seen in the thug Hall, and the fraud side of the novel reaches its climax when he murders Anthony, though another irony of the novel is that it seems from the final pages that Kate remains unaware of this. Hall is a well-drawn minor character who is summed up by the atmosphere he carries with him of 'third-class Pullmans to Brighton, the week-end jaunt, the whisky and splash, peroxide blonde' (p.161). But there is a more sinister side to him in his need for 'blowing off steam' in acts of violence. At the same time, he is said to have a love for Krogh which is 'admirable, pathetic, vicious' (p.190). The result is the calculated murder of Anthony and at this point the novel assumes the aspect of a 'thriller' with Hall as the villain.

ACTIVITY

The whole point of a 'thriller' is to keep the reader in *suspense*, to achieve effects by *surprise*. How might these techniques be seen in relation to Dennis Walder's and Graham Martin's remarks on narrative in Block 2?

DISCUSSION

I am thinking of the way in which Anthony's murder is set up by Hall. He deliberately leaves his note-case at Krogh's poker party, though even Gullie thinks this is uncharacteristic. This, of course, is so that he has a reason to return later, so establishing some form of alibi. Is this not a form of 'internal prolepsis', to use the terms introduced by Dennis Walder? The same effect is then achieved again when Hall does return and Kate asks whether Anthony accompanied him. In the terms used by Graham Martin, the murder is a 'kernel', the note-case incident a 'satellite'.

6 GRAHAM GREENE: 'ENGLAND MADE ME'

BLOCK 3
'ENGLISHNESS'

Greene's prose style in *England Made Me*

ACTIVITY

I have remarked several times already on the experimental nature of Greene's technique in this novel. What links, if any, can you see between Modernism as you encountered it in Block 2 and Greene's way of writing?

DISCUSSION

One of the similarities between the two is the way in which the consciousness of the various characters is presented, and this is reminiscent of techniques Virginia Woolf employs in *Mrs Dalloway*. Anthony's memories of his past life, in the second section of Part I, are in first-person narration which, earlier, I suggested had something in common with 'stream of consciousness' techniques. It is not unlike the way in which we get to learn of Mrs Dalloway's thoughts and feelings at the start of Virginia Woolf's novel.

ACTIVITY

Another link between Modernism and Greene's way of writing is the use of imagery and allusion to bring out one of the book's themes: look, for example, at the use Greene makes of the tiger Anthony wins at the fairground stall (pp.33, 66). What does it allude to, and what is the effect of the allusion?

DISCUSSION

Many of you will have recognized the allusion to William Blake's poem 'The Tyger' in *Songs of Innocence and of Experience* which begins:

> Tyger Tyger, burning bright,
> In the forests of the night;
> What immortal hand or eye,
> Could frame thy fearful symmetry?

As this allusion comes as part of Kate's thoughts about her and her brother's past and present circumstances, and since it is followed by another realization of the (incestuous) love she bears, it could be seen as an emblem, a way of expressing the fusion of good and bad things that go to make up their relationship. There is, I suggest, confirmation for this in the 'toy lamb' that is mentioned a few lines later, for the counterpart to the tiger in *Songs of Innocence* is a lamb. Such a condensed style of writing is often closer to the poet than to the conventional narrative novelist.

6.17   The poet Greene most admired during the 1930s was Auden. In 1937, two years after *England Made Me*, Greene was to describe Auden (in the 'Auden Special Number' of *New Verse*) as the 'finest living poet' in spite of the fact that, ideologically, he was much closer to Eliot at that time, who may, from the point of view of style, have had an influence on both of them. As the critic Bernard Bergonzi has pointed out in an essay 'Auden/Greene' (1978, pp.60–61), it is possible to set lines from a Greene novel as free verse. Take, for example, Anthony's first-person narration on page 19:

> Everybody in bed; the night cold
> And the water invisible under the pale
> Knife-edge of foam. The man in the lower bunk
> Talking all night in a language I do not understand,
> And the new day grey and windy,
> The canvas of the deck chairs flapping,
> And very few people at breakfast;
> An unshaven chin, the dismal jocularity of stewards,
> A girl with hair like Greta Garbo's walking alone,
> A smell of oil and a long time till lunch,
> Kate thinking of Krogh.

6.18 This may not be an especially distinguished piece of verse, but it could probably muster for a piece of descriptive writing in which social observations mix with what Bergonzi calls 'the catalogue'. If you think back to the Auden poems you read earlier in the block, I think you will see what I mean about similarities. Look, for example, at the second stanza of 'Birthday Poem'. Another comparison could be made with an early Eliot poem, 'Preludes':

> The morning comes to consciousness
> Of faint stale smells of beer
> From the sawdust-trampled street
> With all its muddy feet that press
> To early coffee-stands.

6.19 The point that emerges overall is Greene's conscious preoccupation with style at this point in his writing career, and that self-reflexiveness is yet another Modernist trait. It was not to last in his case, as you probably know if you've read any of his other novels, but it does mark *England Made Me* as a novel of its time, the decade of the thirties.

Summary

6.20 The next section of the block is given to poetry by John Betjeman who, you will recall, Greene alludes to when he describes Minty as a 'follower, perhaps, of Sir John Betjeman'. One thing you will be able to take with you from this section is Greene's apparently dismissive view of Minty's religion and its relationship to Englishness. Is this perhaps because, while wanting to hold to the points of the Catholic faith, Minty also wants to hold to his national identity in the form of allegiance to the national church?

ACTIVITY

Before you go on to the next section, jot down what interconnections you see between this section and those earlier. How well is your sense of the block's theme developing as the texts unfold? How central does the E.M. Forster extract in the Reader on English schooling now seem to the block? Does national identity continue to be seen in terms of one gender? Has your sense of the class perspective changed at all as a result of reading Greene's novel? If you think there has been a change, remember to watch to see whether it tips back in the next section. Can you now see connections between Modernism and Block 3? Did Modernism of French and American origin have more links with English writing than is sometimes supposed? These are points to ponder before you go on.

BLOCK 3
'ENGLISHNESS'

7 *John Betjeman*

7.1 In studying Wodehouse's 'Indian Summer of an Uncle' you read (and I hope enjoyed) a text that might be classed by some as belonging to 'popular culture', in the sense that it was written primarily for enjoyment rather than with any great serious purpose. To some extent it could be argued that this is true of Betjeman's poetry, which is undoubtedly popular. As he put it himself:

> I made hay while the sun shone,
> My work sold.

7.2 Betjeman's sense of poetic vocation was both early and strong and, although it was not the career his father would have chosen for him, the paternal advice ('Be funny, John, and be original') was followed to the letter. It made him extraordinarily popular. *Collected Poems* has sold almost 2 million copies which is a huge number by anyone's standards, and at the time of writing the illustrated version of Betjeman's autobiographical poem *Summoned by Bells* is still in the bestseller lists. In addition to his evident popularity with the book-buying public, he was the friend of, and much respected by, Auden, Waugh and Philip Larkin, writers themselves of no little standing. In spite of this, for some critics Betjeman barely exists as a poet, and the amount of critical material on his work is astonishingly meagre.

7.3 Why did the course team choose to devote one section of this block to his work? The reason wasn't to encourage you to debate his status as a twentieth-century writer, though no doubt you will think about this while studying his poetry. He was chosen principally because he allows us to ask interesting questions about the notion of 'Englishness', and that will be the focus of attention in what follows. It is no exaggeration to say that in the course of his life Betjeman became a mascot for the nation. After his death in 1984, *The Times* described him as a 'teddy bear to the nation', picking up on Betjeman's celebrated attachment to his childhood soft toy whom he named Archibald (and wrote a poem about, as we shall see). Indeed, it could be that the public nature of the life he led (at one time a host of television programmes, and always in the news) was one of the reasons he wasn't taken seriously as a poet by some critics and academics. It may be that a proper reassessment of his contribution to modern English poetry is possible only after his death.

7.4 In this section, we shall examine poems from all periods of Betjeman's life because, although the chronological location of Block 3 has been set in the 1930s, Betjeman's work didn't change fundamentally from the first collection in 1932 to the last in 1982. Noting that date, 1932, which was when the first collection, *Mount Zion* (subtitled *In touch with the infinite*), was published, serves to remind us that Betjeman *was* of the 'Auden generation', though he gets no mention in the well-known book of that title by the American critic Samuel Hynes. He was, in fact, born in the same year as Auden.

ACTIVITY

Bearing in mind your work on Auden in Section 4 (glance back to it if necessary), please now turn to the first of Betjeman's poems printed in the Poetry Anthology, 'Death in Leamington' (from *Mount Zion*, 1932). Do you see anything in common with Auden's work? How does the poem compare with others you have read from the 1930s? Does it seem to you to demonstrate a particular version of 'Englishness'?

DISCUSSION

I would argue that there is more in common between Betjeman and Auden than is often supposed. During the thirties, Auden wrote a poem not unlike 'Death in Leamington' called 'Miss Gee' about a woman who, like Betjeman's character, dies. I shall quote just a few lines to show you what I mean:

> Let me tell you a little story. About Miss Edith Gee:
> She lived in Clevedon Terrace. At Number 83.

Like two of the poems mentioned in Section 4 ('Now the leaves are falling fast', 'O what is that sound') 'Death in Leamington' has a pronounced rhyme and rhythm. Despite these similarities the two poets diverge, I would argue, over the issue of politics. As you will have realized from Section 4 and from the interviews in TV5 *Left and Write*, the 1930s was an intensely political decade in which, as Julian Symons and Stephen Spender made clear, most writers felt compelled to take up a position of some kind. A poem like 'A Summer Night' is, among other things, openly about European politics; one stanza refers explicitly to Poland's 'Eastern bow'. There is no hint of this at all in Betjeman's work in the 1930s. You would never guess from the poems in *Mount Zion* that Europe was in a state of intense crisis. (This may be one reason why Betjeman hasn't been taken seriously by many critics and writers on the decade such as Samuel Hynes.) In fact, *Mount Zion*, with its peculiar subtitle and illustrations (one of a woman speaking into an old-fashioned telephone), is rather consciously detached from the concerns of this world. Several of the poems in the short collections are concerned, like 'Death in Leamington', with death and the fate of the human soul.

There are, I think, a number of qualities in 'Death in Leamington' that establish an English sense of identity. For a start, there is the title: the narrative of the poem is set specifically in an English country town, one known for its spa (and so associated with sickness). Then there is an air of gentility appropriate to suburbia – the woman crochets and has afternoon tea, and when she is discovered to be dead, the lamp is lowered as an outward sign of respect. Most telling of all is the line

> Oh! Chintzy, chintzy cheeriness,

which has entered the language (for a certain section of society) as a wonderfully plangent phrase, redolent of nostalgia and affection, which describes not simply a style of furnishing but a whole way of life. (Angus Calder illustrates aspects of this life without actually quoting this poem in TV4 *Crossing the Border*).

Perhaps the most difficult aspect of the poem is deciding whether it is meant to be serious or amusing. Is Betjeman making fun of the woman (or 'lady', perhaps, in this case)? Is death really a subject for fun? Some of its readers, like Philip Larkin and his friends at Oxford in the 1940s, found it funny, though Larkin, like Betjeman, had a profound fear of death. Is Betjeman making death a subject of fun, perhaps, in order to rob it of its terrors?

ACTIVITY

The theme of suburbia is continued in 'Slough' (from *Continual Dew*, 1937) which Angus Calder discusses in TV4 *Crossing the Border*. Please read it now. Does it shock you and, if so, why? Does it have a message? How does it add to a version of Englishness?

DISCUSSION

The first line is undoubtedly a surprise – how can a bomb possibly be 'friendly'? Initial shock is perhaps tempered by remembering that this poem was written *before* the aerial bombardment of the Second World War. Nevertheless, the memorable 'invitation' both creates and expresses a sense of outrage, a real anger, at what has been done to an English town. (Note again the title.) The speaker (presumably Betjeman or someone who shares most of his views) saves his venom for the perpetrator of the vandalism, the 'man with the double chin' who shamelessly exploits women. The 'bald young clerks' and their wives with 'peroxide hair' he exonerates on the grounds that:

> It's not their fault that they are mad,
> They've tasted Hell.

This is the unambiguous 'message' – that the town has been ruined by profit-seeking developers who have built cheap houses and factories and encouraged a general growth of synthetic goods, themselves a sign of a way of life that is superficial and artificial. How does this fit in with an idea of Englishness? Mainly, I think, through the idea we met in Section 1, that the real England is pastoral. Look at the last stanza again: rescue is to come, when the town has been razed, by new farms in which the earth is allowed to breath again, and fresh food is allowed to grow.

7.5 I want to pursue the definition of Englishness from a slightly different angle by turning to a later poem, 'How to Get On in Society', which was originally a response to a competition in the *New Statesman* (the subtitle is incorrect and misleading). The competition consisted of working into a poem as many 'social solecisms' as possible. Of course, what constitutes a 'social solecism', or *faux-pas*, will depend entirely on your upbringing and the agreed set of rules you assent to in your life in society. As far as this poem is concerned, these issues are entirely class-related and that is why it is useful for the thematic purposes of the block.

ACTIVITY

Please now read the poem and listen to Betjeman's recording of it which is on Audio-cassette 2 Side 1. What 'vulgarities' do you think Betjeman intended to ridicule? (This is not a 'test' but a serious enquiry!)

DISCUSSION

After consulting with colleagues, I came up with this list of what one of them called 'poisonous distinctions':

> 'phone' is slang; 'fish knives', like 'cruets', food with 'frills' and 'forks' for pastries, are examples of attempts at a particular kind of middle-class gentility; 'Norman' (in England at least) is a working-class name; 'kiddies' is slang usage; 'serviettes' is common usage for 'napkins'; 'requisites' is a euphemism; 'toilet' is common usage for lavatory/w.c./loo; the 'logs' are artificial; 'ever so' is slang, as is 'comfy' and 'just as it comes'; a 'lounge' is for those without a drawing-room; 'sweet' is common usage for what others call 'dessert'.

7.6 For the poem to make proper sense you need to know that, at about the time of the competition, a social game was being played by, among others, Nancy Mitford and Alan Ross which consisted of defining behaviour which was 'U' and 'non-U' – that is, acceptable and unacceptable to 'upper-class society', or the kind of groups that Waugh and Betjeman, both snobs in their own ways, aspired to join. The relevance of the theme for this block hardly needs pointing out: we are back with the English obsession with social class.

ACTIVITY

There is quite a lot about class in Betjeman's poetry: look now, for example, at 'Hunter Trials' in the Poetry Anthology (from *A Few Late Chrysanthemums*, 1954). Apart from the interest of this poem to the theme of Englishness, try to define what makes it amusing (if you think it is). (Betjeman reads it on Audio-cassette 2 Side 1.)

DISCUSSION

The relevance to the theme, I suggest, is that both the speech patterns and the activity (girls on their ponies) are related to the more moneyed and leisured members of English society. The first line is cast in a particular class dialect in which certain syllables are elided. The discourse of the poem is cast in the voice of an enthusiastic young horse-mad girl who is thrown by 'Smudges' and breaks her collarbone. The horse's name is an example of one source of humour, which is that the poem is full of unusual and inappropriate names: 'Guzzle', 'Mrs Geyser', 'Mona Lisa', 'Miss Blewitt', and so on. The other technique Betjeman uses is incongruity: setting one thing unexpectedly next to another, thus achieving the effect of surprise. For example, it's patently ridiculous to imagine a girl trying to retrieve something from a pony's stomach using a spanner, if the creature were to have done something as unlikely as to swallow its 'bits' in the first place; then there is the pun on bit/'bits'. It's equally absurd (though not altogether improbable) for the young rider to dismiss her accident as 'my silly old collarbone's bust', so the overall effect is that the reader tends not to take the events of the poem seriously. Yet it has, besides the class issue, another interesting feature.

ACTIVITY

Recalling Angus Calder's discussion of Wodehouse's story in Section 3, how would you describe the world Betjeman depicts in the poem in terms of gender?

DISCUSSION

What struck me was that the world of this poem is intensely female – girls and a mother who is twice addressed by her daughter. Yet, at the same time, it has a robust atmosphere which seems more a male than a female quality – intense physical activity and dismissing injury as something of little consequence.

ACTIVITY

This suggestion of 'cross-gendering' is to be found in other poems: please now read 'The Olympic Girl' (from *A Few Late Chrysanthemums*, 1954). (You can hear a version of it set to music on Audio-cassette 2 Side 1.) How would you

BLOCK 3 'ENGLISHNESS'

describe the relationship in this poem, and what attitudes are behind it? Does it add to the account of Englishness in any way? (The Greek phrase, incidentally, simply anticipates the end of the line and means 'as it were'.)

DISCUSSION

The speaker seems to have a poor opinion of himself, however humorously it is expressed: he is an 'unhealthy worm' beside her 'strong, athletic pose'. It is the 'fair tigress' who is the source of energy and activity. Imagining himself her racket – in other words, her instrument – the hapless admirer is drawn into intimacy by *her* vigour and energy, yet in her distance she remains 'Olympic' in more senses than one. By comparison, as I point out on Audio-cassette 2 Side 1, he emerges as essentially passive, even rather weak. Yet his position is rescued from being merely pitiable by the fact that he can laugh at himself and turn the occasion into humour. Humour is notoriously difficult to 'explain' and it does seem to have national qualities (for example, Americans need the cartoons in *Punch* explained to them). 'English' humour has often been seen as a way of the nation laughing at itself, and, like many other nations, in a self-deprecating way; the male character in 'The Olympic Girl' is perhaps an individual example of this. The Englishness theme is sustained by the reference to Rupert Brooke, author of the celebrated lines about England and his death quoted by Graham Martin in Block 1 Section 4.

> If I should die, think only this of me:
>   That there's some corner of a foreign field
> That is for ever England. There shall be
>   In that rich earth a richer dust concealed;
> A dust whom England bore, shaped, made aware,
>   Gave, once, her flowers to love, her ways to roam,
> A body of England's, breathing English air,
>   Washed by the rivers, blest by suns of home.

ACTIVITY

The gender issue in relationships emerges in a slightly different way in an earlier poem, 'A Subaltern's Love-song' (from *New Bats in Old Belfries*, 1945, reprinted in the Poetry Anthology). Please read it now and listen to Betjeman's rendition of it on Audio-cassette 2 Side 1. Does it have anything in common with 'The Olympic Girl'? How does it differ? What sort of world do this pair live in?

DISCUSSION

Like 'The Olympic Girl' it is, in the first few stanzas, about a tennis match between a young girl and an admiring man. Again, it is the woman who seems to have the male qualities – she is 'burnish'd by Aldershot sun' and has 'the grace of a boy'. (Aldershot, the primary army-officer training centre, has strong military, that is, male, associations, yet the man in the relationship is specifically given the *junior* rank of 'subaltern', so his inferiority is even expressed in formal terms.) The match is seen as a contest between the two rather than a game and it is Miss J. Hunter Dunn who wins, having reduced her opponent to a state of weakness (see stanza 2). Yet her victory produces mixed feelings in her opponent because he is, he says, in love with her and this love is reciprocated. In this the poem differs from 'The Olympic Girl'. The second part of the poem describes how the couple spend the rest of the day, finally becoming engaged to marry. Yet it is Miss J. Hunter Dunn who remains firmly in charge of the situation – note that it is she who is 'on my right', in the driver's seat in the car, and one wonders, perhaps, who proposed to whom.

The subaltern is clearly a house-guest of the Hunter Dunns, who seem to lead a stockbroker-belt life with material comforts to hand. Like many of Betjeman's poems, the setting is placed very firmly in a recognizable, English context: the brand names of the cars are known to all, Camberley and Surrey are evoked memorably and economically in just four lines. (Even Miss J. Hunter Dunn's name, being double-barrelled, suggests something 'upper class', or perhaps 'rising middle-class'.) The economy of Betjeman's technique is impressive: note the clever internal rhyme of the second and third stanzas and the apparently effortless way he swings from stanza to stanza in ingeniously formed iambic pentameters.

7.7 Yet in all other respects Betjeman's world is that of pre-war days. 'The Olympic Girl' demonstrates his apparent lack of interest in writing about the world of war and politics. Waugh, a shrewd critic of other writers' work, admired Betjeman as a poet who had contributed 'four or five poems to that undefinable and extremely limited anthology which every educated Englishman carries in his memory'. (Note the *national* and *gender* restriction again – what does the educated English woman carry in *her* memory?) Yet there was one topic on which they diverged sharply, namely religious denomination. Waugh, you will recall from Radio 4 *Home and Abroad*, was received into the Roman Catholic Church in 1930, a decision to which he remained unswervingly committed until the end of his life. He was not unmindful of his apostolic duty to others and, according to his second wife, was at least partly responsible for Frank (later Lord) Longford's decision to become a Catholic. He may well have played a part, too, in the conversion of Betjeman's wife Penelope, for they corresponded about it. Penelope's eventual decision caused Betjeman distress because, as she explained to Waugh:

> [John] thinks ROMAN Catholicism is a foreign religion which has no right to set up in this country, let alone try to make converts from what he regards as the true Catholic church of this country.
> (Amory, 1982, p.250)

7.8 Waugh had accused Betjeman of 'perpetuating a sixteenth-century rift and influencing others to perpetuate it', to which he had replied:

> It would be far *easier* (but against my conscience) to become R.C. For in this village ... the only bulwark against complete paganism is the Church and its chief supporters are Penelope and me...
> (Amory, 1982, p.250, n.3)

7.9 Anglicanism was deeply associated in Betjeman's mind with a sense of his national identity, though to Waugh his reasoning was completely faulty. Waugh's view of Betjeman's religious position, however unfair, was analogous to Greene's depiction of Minty's Anglo-Catholicism in *England Made Me* – something which couldn't be taken quite seriously.

7.10 Leaving theological differences aside, however, religion was clearly important to Betjeman, demonstrated by the number of poems he wrote about it. The titles alone are evidence of this: 'An Eighteenth-century Calvinistic Hymn', 'Our Padre', 'Undenominational', 'Olney Hymns', 'Lenten Thought of a High Anglican', 'An Ecumenical Invitation'. The latter, written in the wake of the changes in the Catholic Church in the 1960s, and written in the voice of a patronizing Catholic mother, gave Betjeman an opportunity to get his own back on Waugh in these lines:

> I never liked that term 'non-Catholic' –
> The word we used to use for Anglicans,
> Though several of my really greatest friends
> Were once non-Catholics – take Evelyn Waugh
> (God rest his soul!) and Graham Sutherland;

7.11 It would be misleading to describe Betjeman as a 'religious' poet in the sense that the Eliot of *Four Quartets* might be, though there seems little reason to doubt, on the basis of such poems as 'Christmas', that he was anything but a convinced member of the Church of England (unlike Philip Larkin who described himself as an 'unbelieving' member of the same institution). 'Christmas' ends with these lines:

> No love that in a family dwells,
>   No carolling in frosty air
> Nor all the steeple-shaking bells
>   Can with this single Truth compare –
> That God was man in Palestine
> And lives today in Bread and Wine.

and, in a television film made in 1976, Betjeman is seen genuflecting as he revisits Pusey House in Oxford where he used to worship.

7.12 This serious side to the 'court jester' poet was perhaps related to his fear of death, which itself might have had its origin in the tales of hell told him in childhood by one particularly neurotic nursemaid in whose hands he suffered. He turned, so he tells his readers, to his teddy bear for comfort.

ACTIVITY

The bear, Archibald, has acquired a certain notoriety. Please now read the poem with that title in the Poetry Anthology. Who is speaking in the poem? What strikes you as unusual about it?

DISCUSSION

The speaker, we find out halfway through, is the poet in middle age talking to his childhood bear. In the first stanzas, he thinks back to his childhood ('Thirty One West Hill' was where the family lived in Highgate, north London, and Cornwall was where they took their annual holidays), and the bear seems to be repeating his nurse's words to him. He remembers, at the age of nine, fearing his father's disapproval of this attachment which then becomes a 'guilty passion'. In the second part of the poem, the bear becomes the one constant, unchanging thing in the world which he can cling to as memories of the years rush past. Finally, recognizing that a psychiatrist would find this attachment to a childhood toy somewhat unusual in an adult man, he expresses his real fear: that deprival would bring about an endless emptiness to his life. Some critics have found this wholly risible and seized on the poem as an opportunity to ridicule Betjeman. Others, trained in the school of Freud and his disciples, have seen it as an expression of arrested development, of failure to grow out of dependence on what the psychiatrist D.W. Winnicot has called a 'transitional object' – one that the child uses to relate his/her identity to the outside world. Betjeman seems to see something of this himself in the final stanza, and there may be some truth in the observation. But, more simply, it could also be that the poem is an expression of the black depressions Betjeman suffered from.

7.13 'Archibald' makes some reference to the poet's childhood, which was, of course, in part the subject of his long autobiographical poem *Summoned by Bells*. The poem treats only the poet's early years but, as he recognizes, they were formative and perhaps explain some of his aspirations and behaviour in later life. Betjeman's biographer, Bevis Hillier, has recently revealed the astonishing fact that the late Hugh Gaitskell (leader of the Labour Party, 1955–63), a fellow pupil at Marlborough School, was not allowed to visit Betjeman in the holidays because Betjeman's father was 'in trade': the young poet had an early schooling in the fine social distinctions which he was so carefully to observe and record in his poetry and which have so long been part of the English way of life.

ACTIVITY

What English qualities do you see in 'Mortality' (from *High and Low*, 1966, reprinted in the Poetry Anthology), and how (if it does) does it modify your view of the kind of poet Betjeman is? What emotion do you detect behind it? Please read it now and listen to Betjeman's version of it on Audio-cassette 2 Side 1.

DISCUSSION

In some ways 'Mortality' (like 'Slough') is really rather a vicious poem and does much to vitiate the idea of Betjeman as a comfortable poet of 'whimsy' and triviality, for the narrator seems to take positive pleasure in the violent end of a senior civil servant. The particular 'English' quality I had in mind is the spirit of endless compromise that the civil servant seems to embody, and also the whole system of rewards and class he represents (a 'K', of course, is a knighthood in the honours list). The over-judicious, bureaucratic spirit of compromise, thought by some to be one of the better characteristics of the English, is one that appears to enrage the poet. I have the sense that, in addition to being 'black comedy', there is much anger in this poem. This quality (which Larkin noted) is perhaps more common in Betjeman's work than is ever supposed, though he was well known in public life for his spirited defence of causes he believed in, like the preservation of Victorian railway stations. Could it be that in this poem he has in mind some of the people he dealt with in the course of his public work?

ACTIVITY

The last poem I would like you to look at is 'The Arrest of Oscar Wilde at the Cadogan Hotel' (from *Continual Dew*, 1937). Wilde, the nineteenth-century wit and playwright, was being arrested for an illegal homosexual relationship. What do you think Betjeman was aiming to achieve in this poem, and how does it add to the theme of this block?

DISCUSSION

It seems to me in part another expression of Betjeman's interest in things Victorian: notice how precise he is about the architecture of Pont Street and the gaslight shining in through the window. He creates a vignette of a scene in Wilde's life and, in the process, economically evokes a whole decade – the 1890s of the *Yellow Book* period. Wilde has 'bees-winged eyes' and is, presumably, drinking his hock and seltzer as a hangover cure. Nowhere is the reason for the arrest even hinted at – Betjeman assumes that this notorious incident in English legal history, resulting in Wilde's imprisonment and subsequent composition of 'The Ballad of Reading Gaol', will be known to his readers.

I think the poem relates to the theme of this block in several ways. Firstly, it refers implicitly to homosexuality, and also to English hypocrisy over sexual behaviour. Secondly, there is the entry of the comic policemen with their cockney accents who, to preserve propriety, ask Wilde to go quietly. Class and dialect emerge again, but this time from lower down the social ladder. Does Betjeman mean the reader to be amused by the poem? The answer, I think, is yes – why otherwise would he play around with the typeface when announcing the arrival of the police? But it is a form of black comedy, for Wilde's position was indeed serious. Betjeman's first intention was, I think, to 'be funny', as his father had advised. It is an interesting poem technically: though in a familiar stanza form, skilled use is made of rhyme (only two rhymes in each four-line stanza) as the speaker moves easily from narrative to dialogue.

ACTIVITY

I said at the beginning of this section that my aim was not to attempt a general assessment of Betjeman's status or provide a general study of his work. Nevertheless, there is a value in considering his work not just in the context of the 1930s but also in relation to Modernism. How does Betjeman's work stand in relation to Modernism?

DISCUSSION

If you applied the criteria of the characteristics Graham Martin mentioned in Block 2 – work that is self-referential, full of allusions and highly concerned with the manner of its own expression – you might think that Betjeman's work has absolutely nothing in common with the Modernist poets. Betjeman's work, your first thought might be, is 'accessible', which is one reason for its popularity. You might also argue that in this it is also characteristically 'English', that Modernism was something which took its origin in nineteenth-century France and was imposed on English culture by two Americans. To a great extent this is undeniable, yet the critic Andrew Motion has argued (in a BBC television programme, *Eliot and After*, November 1988) that there is common ground, and that Betjeman could be seen as the meeting point between Modernism and the native tradition of English poetry. Angus Calder has pointed out that Betjeman 'plays on the English acceptance of, and delight in middle-class eccentricity' and comments:

> He's as close to Stevie Smith as he is to Auden. There is a long *tradition* of English 'comic' verse ... this 'lightness' is widespread in English writing and seems to me characteristically 'English'. Crucially, Betjeman can *get away with* the sadistic implications of 'Slough' or 'Mortality' because these can be seen as products of 'Ealing comedy' eccentricity.

Think about this particular kind of Englishness for a moment. Is it one you recognize? Is it class related? You will need to consider this in the next section of the block where the text is a novel by Betjeman's friend and admirer, Evelyn Waugh. Angus Calder suggests that the quality of anachronism which is undeniably a part of Betjeman's poetry, or can be seen to be, is another version of the 'displacement' that characterizes Modernist verse. I think this is an argument that will take you only so far, for the truth seems to be that Betjeman is extraordinarily difficult to pin down in terms of other people's poetry, though his fondness for Tennyson and other Victorian poets is no secret or surprise. If you try to describe him in terms simply of 'whimsy' or 'pastiche', what do you do with a poem like 'Mortality'? Has he paid a price for his eventual popularity, thereby losing another audience, one that perceives being an 'entertainer' and a 'serious poet' as an incompatible combination? Would this have mattered to him? What was his contribution to English poetry, and was it only to *English* poetry? Will he be read by future generations, or by those who don't share his sympathies? These are questions for you to think about before going on to the next section.

8 Evelyn Waugh: 'Officers and Gentlemen'

8.1 *Officers and Gentlemen* is the second novel in a trilogy by Evelyn Waugh which looks back over British involvement in the Second World War. The first is called *Men at Arms*. The fact that it is the 'middle section' of a longer work does not present any particular difficulties because each novel was published independently and intended to be read as such. Indeed, at the time *Officers and Gentlemen* was published there was no certainty that there would be a third novel. After its eventual appearance in 1961 as *Unconditional Surrender*, Waugh decided to put all three together, with certain editorial changes, under the title *Sword of Honour*, a reference to two swords, one ancient, one modern, which feature in the course of the narrative. 'Honour' – what it is, why it is important – features prominently in *Officers and Gentlemen* and is one of the running themes in the trilogy as a whole.

8.2 The principal character in all three novels – I won't say hero for reasons that will become clear – is Guy Crouchback, a diffident man in his thirties from an old landed recusant Catholic family, who has been married to a woman named Virginia but, at the beginning of *Men at Arms*, is divorced. He has been living in Italy until the outbreak of the war, when, on the signing of the German-Russian pact of non-aggression in 1939, he decides to seek a commission 'to serve his King'. For Guy, it seems an opportunity to repair his life after 'eight years of shame and loneliness', for

> The enemy at last was plain in view, huge and hateful, all disguise off. It was the Modern Age in arms. Whatever the outcome there was a place for him in that battle.
>
> (*Men at Arms*, p.12)

8.3 *Men at Arms* tells how Guy gets his commission in the Halberdiers regiment and goes through training in the company of assorted characters, most notably one named Apthorpe whose death concludes the first novel. Guy had been indirectly involved in this by providing Apthorpe with forbidden whisky. As a result of this and a discreditable incident he is involved in at Dakar, he is consequently posted out of the recently formed second battalion of the Halberdiers.

8.4 The beginning of the second novel, *Officers and Gentlemen*, finds him outside his London club at the beginning of an air raid during the blitz after Dunkirk in late 1940. The end of the novel is set in the summer of 1941, after the withdrawal of the Allies from the island of Crete, so the action takes place over a period of roughly twelve months. Guy is waiting for a posting at the start of *Officers and Gentlemen*, and he has some unfinished business from *Men at Arms*: he has to dispose of the belongings of the deceased Apthorpe to whom he made such a promise.

BLOCK 3 'ENGLISHNESS'

8.5 Inevitably in a novel set in wartime with an army officer as its main character, there are a great number of references to military practice and the use of a number of terms and initials which will make sense only to the initiated. For example, 'blue jobs' to an army officer means someone in the navy because of the colour of their uniforms; conversely, to the navy the army are 'brown jobs'. But you don't need an informed awareness of exactly what a brigade, or a subaltern, or a platoon is to make sense of the novel because the meaning emerges sufficiently from the context for the purposes of the narrative. Nevertheless, you might consider the extent to which *Officers and Gentlemen* could be said to be 'about' the army and its customs. Bear this in mind as you read. Ask yourself as well whether it could be called a 'war novel'. If it could, then what is its relationship with history? For the blitz and the German invasion of Crete which feature in the novel are fact not fiction.

8.6 The main question to keep in mind, however, is the subject of Block 3 – 'Englishness'. In what ways can 'Englishness' be discerned in the pages of the novel? How is the block theme related to the discussion of values and ethics? What lesson does Guy learn by the end of the novel? Is it related to a political or religious position? And, if it is, does this limit the appeal of the work to a certain audience? (To some extent these are questions of *interpretation* – the subject of the final section of this block. Raising them here in relation to a particular text is a prelude to the discussion of the *theory of interpretation* in Section 9.)

8.7 Now a word about the structure of *Officers and Gentlemen*. As you will see from the contents page of the Penguin edition, it is cast as two books with an interlude between them and an epilogue. Within each book there are numbered episodes, each distinct in place and incident. From the opening pages you will also notice that Waugh employs a lot of dialogue so that the overall effect often resembles that of film. As in a film, the reader is called on to work out what is happening under the surface of events which need interpreting. With Guy, the principal character, a lot of this is done for us by Waugh: in Cohn's terms, by *psycho-narration* of the *consonant* kind in the third person narrative. Writing in this episodic medium where place and characters are constantly switching can sometimes be a little tricky to review when you come to write about the novel. I suggest that, for Book One, you try jotting down a one line summary of what happens in each section. This should not take long, and at the end of your reading you will have a handy guide to the start of the novel to use for discussion purposes.

8.8 Please now read Book One 'Happy Warriors' and then compare your summary of events with mine on pages 104–6. Grasping what takes place is my main concern at this point. I shall come back to other issues later. Waugh writes with great economy, so a certain amount of 'unpicking' is necessary.

8.9 Now read right through to the end of the novel without interruption. After the Interlude, which is set in Cape Town in February 1941, the rest of the novel pivots on two actions, 'Operation Popgun' involving Trimmer, and the invasion of Crete involving Guy. 'Popgun' is, of course, fiction, but the Cretan episode was a significant episode in the Second World War. (You don't need a detailed knowledge of the history of the war to follow it.)

ACTIVITY

What sort of novel is *Officers and Gentlemen*? Let us look at the options: is it a 'war novel'?

DISCUSSION

In one sense it clearly is a 'war' novel, for the whole action takes place in the middle of the Second World War and one of its significant episodes on Crete is looked at in some detail. On the other hand, the progress of the war as a whole is obviously not Waugh's subject, which is why Book Two makes sense to a reader with only a limited knowledge of the history of the time. Nor is he concerned with details of military action beyond what is necessary for the plot, nor with military equipment.

ACTIVITY

Remembering that Waugh was writing in 1953 of events that took place in 1941, is it in any sense an 'historical novel'?

DISCUSSION

I would hesitate to call it this myself because 'historical' implies something set before the author's lifetime, a period recreated with care through historical research. For *Officers and Gentlemen* Waugh was calling on his own memory and those of others: you may have noticed the complimentary dedication to Major-General Sir Robert Laycock at the start of the novel. Laycock was the man to whom Waugh acted as personal assistant during the action in Crete in 1941 (and one of the few of his commanding officers who did not dislike him as a soldier). The authenticity and vividness of Book Two, Sections 4, 5 and 6, are the result of Waugh drawing on his own experience and the diary which he, like many others, kept (illegally) at the time. Perhaps, then, *Officers and Gentlemen* could be called *historical*, though not in the sense that Sir Walter Scott's novels are.

ACTIVITY

Does this mean, then, that *Officers and Gentlemen* is an 'autobiographical' novel?

DISCUSSION

Since Waugh draws on his own experience (as his diaries for 1941 show) and since the principal character is a Roman Catholic who becomes progressively disillusioned with the world (in this respect perhaps like himself), the temptation may be to say 'yes'. But I think it should be resisted. All writers draw in various ways on their own experience, which is then used or mediated through the artistic process into something different. In this case, although the events of the novel are (according to Waugh's friend and biographer Christopher Sykes) true to the facts, the human side was quite different. For one thing, Waugh was happily married with a young family; for another, he was very unpopular with his men, who would not obey his orders, whereas the divorced and unhappy Guy is a model officer in his handling of the 'ranks'.

ACTIVITY

Since much of the novel is concerned with the army, could it be described as a 'military' novel?

DISCUSSION

To a degree I think perhaps it might. There is, for example, the title. Though not without its ironical connotations (which I shall come to shortly), both Waugh's original idea for the title, *Happy Warriors*, and the later American suggestion which he accepted, *Officers and Gentlemen*, indicate that this is to be an account of the life of the British officer class. The title states clearly the particular limits Waugh set himself: there is no attempt to see army life from the point of view of the conscript or ordinary serving soldier. The closest Waugh comes to this is with the NCO Corporal-Major Ludovic, who is capable on occasions of resorting to his native demotic speech as he does in Book 2, Section 6, when he tells Hound to 'Shut your bloody trap'. But the eccentric and sinister Ludovic cannot be seen in any way as representative. In this middle novel of the trilogy in particular, Waugh's principal characters are all commissioned officers with a shared code of conduct and manner of speech, and one is a peer of the realm as well.

Then there is the depiction of everyday life in the army itself, unmistakably a British institution and an emblem of the national culture. (A little caution is necessary here, for though our theme is 'Englishness', the army is of course a *British* institution.) Waugh was clearly fascinated (at least initially) by the army with its intricate procedures, its laws and structure, its complex set of relationships. According to his friend Harold Acton (interviewed in a BBC television programme, *Arena*, in 1987), Waugh needed institutions like the church and the army because he was naturally undisciplined and anarchistic, and so rejoiced in their insistence on legality of procedure.

There are many examples of army style in *Officers and Gentlemen*: take, for example, Book One, Section 7, where Tommy Blackhouse and Guy go to dine with the Laird of Mugg. Tommy is now Guy's commanding officer, though they have known each other for many years and, indeed, have both been married to Virginia, a fact which we are told bonds them: 'Men who have loved the same woman are blood brothers even in enmity' (p.68). Moreover, 'If they laugh together, as Tommy and Guy laughed that night, orgiastically, they seal their friendship on a plane rarer and loftier than normal human intercourse' (p.68). Yet the very next day the relationship between the two men changes when a message comes from HOO HQ that Guy remains the 'personal property of Colonel Ritchie-Hook' and is not to be one of Tommy Blackhouse's men: 'Last night they had been close friends. Today they were Colonel and Subaltern' (p.71). Guy now becomes simply a junior officer, and he reflects on the suddenness of this transformation: 'In all his military service Guy never ceased to marvel at the effortless transitions of intercourse between equality and superiority' (p.70).

Another aspect of army life which clearly intrigued Waugh was how to know the limits of what you could expect to 'get away with'. There are clearly delicate nuances to this knowledge which the professional soldier like Jumbo Trotter possesses intuitively. When helping to move Apthorpe's belongings, Jumbo is asked whether a label can be illicitly affixed to their car to smooth their passage: '"Why not?" he said. But he thought again. Reason regained its sway. He drew from the deep source of his military experience and knew to a finger's breadth how far one could go. "No," he said regretfully. "That wouldn't do"' (p.46).

Major Hound, on the other hand, whom we first meet in Book Two, Section 1, goes to the other extreme in his insistence on doing everything by the book and his conviction that, even in the most dire situation, there must be a 'staff solution'.

Lastly, there is the ceremonial activity and formality associated with regimental life, another characteristic thought to be particularly English. In fact, there is less emphasis on this in *Officers and Gentlemen* than in *Men at Arms*, where Guy joins the Halberdiers and goes through a period of initiation, learning the particular traditions and customs of his regiment. We meet this again in the closing pages of *Officers and Gentlemen* where Guy reports back to the Captain-Commandant and has to be found a pair of gloves before he is properly dressed. Also, he is made aware that it 'was not the business of a Halberdier officer to get his name in the papers' even though his 'exploit had been wholly creditable' (p.248). You may have noted, too, that in the withdrawal from Crete it is only Halberdier officers who show a recognizable degree of order amid the surrounding chaos. The novel closes with an affectionate, if perhaps sentimental, acknowledgement to the colour-sergeant of the regiment, and the regiment is consistently portrayed in a favourable light.

8 EVELYN WAUGH: 'OFFICERS AND GENTLEMEN'

8.10 Officers and Gentlemen is difficult to categorize since it displays characteristics of various types of fiction: serious in purpose it is also very funny in places, and it is this mixture of qualities that makes it unusual and memorable.

Officers *and* gentlemen?

ACTIVITY

Let us consider certain specific aspects and themes of Waugh's novel. Taking up the army theme, what does it have to say about 'officers' and their claim to be 'gentlemen'?

DISCUSSION

The assumption behind the phrase is that the two are synonymous – an officer is always a gentleman, though the reverse is not necessarily true, of course. This is not always the case, though, as this old joke makes clear:

> DÉBUTANTE TO NOUVEAU RICHE FATHER   Daddy, I've fallen in love with an officer and a gentleman.
>
> DADDY   Bring them both round to tea, and we'll sort it out.

But what does the word 'gentleman' mean? According to the *OED* it can mean a number of things: originally it meant a man of gentle birth, that is, in terms of the British class system, one 'entitled to bear arms, though not noble'. In 1463 it had come to mean 'a person of rank'. By 1862 it was being used in legal documents to mean someone who 'had no occupation', who didn't have to work for a living. More recently, it has designated 'a man of money and leisure'. Generally, without specific reference to rank or class, it has been used to mean a man of 'chivalrous instincts and fine feelings', as in that richly encoded saying, 'he's one of nature's gentlemen'. Decoded, I take this to mean that possessing good manners is normally the prerogative of belonging to a certain 'class' but that, exceptionally, people of humble origins may display courtesy. Is Waugh, then, implying by his title that:

(a)   officers all come from a certain socio-economic class;

(b)   that all officers will act like gentlemen?

Proposition (a) is generally true, as we have seen, though with exceptions. Proposition (b) is much more doubtful and Waugh's use of the phrase for his title is surely meant to be heavily ironic. Miss Vavasour has raised the issue in Book One, Section 3, over the visit of the Quartering Commandant Grigshawe to the Marine Hotel.

BLOCK 3
'ENGLISHNESS'

ACTIVITY

Would you now analyse the whole episode over old Mr Crouchback's rooms in terms of class implications? What can you disinter from the text about the attitudes *of* and *to* the characters involved?

DISCUSSION

Miss Vavasour tells Mr Crouchback: 'There was an officer here today – at least he was dressed as an officer – a dreadful sort of person' (p.23). She then goes on with her story: the Cuthberts who run the hotel have described Mr Crouchback as simply 'a schoolteacher' in a private school, at which 'the officer laughed and said "Priority nil"'. When Mr Crouchback attempts to calm her, she comes back with the reply: 'You are too trustful, Mr Crouchback. You treat everyone as if he were a gentleman. That officer definitely was *not.*'

The conclusion of the episode comes in the next section with the arrival of Jumbo Trotter who recognizes Grigshawe as one of his regiment's former drill-sergeants, now with an acting rank as an officer. Trotter's comment on this promotion is revealing: 'What, Grigshawe? One of the best drill-sergeants we had in the Corps. Extraordinary system taking first-rate NCOs and making second-rate officers of them' (p.35).

There is throughout these scenes in the Marine Hotel a strong sense of class-resentments and misunderstandings of a peculiarly English kind. Miss Vavasour resents the fact that Mr Crouchback is not recognized for *'who you are'*, that is, from an old landed gentry family and therefore socially superior to most of the other residents. Trotter clearly thinks that Grigshawe, who laughs at the notion of a *private* education, is not 'officer material'. The Cuthberts, who resent losing the chance of making more money out of Mr Crouchback's second room, are seen as grasping and mean-minded: Jumbo Trotter sees Mrs Cuthbert as 'the poor type' just as in his private classification he recognizes Mr Crouchback as: '"a good type"; not only the father of a Halberdier but a man fit to be a Halberdier himself' (p.36).

The Cuthberts do not emerge well from these scenes: thinking they had formed a class alliance with Grigshawe ('everything seemed so friendly'), they feel let down when Trotter intervenes, and they put it down to Mr Crouchback, who has: 'seen better days … There's something about people like him. They were brought up to expect things to be easy for them and somehow or other things always *are* easy. Damned if I know how they manage it' (p.38).

But the *coup de grâce* for the Cuthberts is shortly to follow when Mr Crouchback enters and offers them his sitting-room to let to someone else. Mr Crouchback's noble act of sacrifice elicits a baffled response from the Cuthberts: 'He's a deep one and no mistake. I never have understood him, not properly. Somehow his mind seems to work different from yours and mine' (p.38). The enormity of the gap between them is emphasized by the grammatical error which, in a prose as correct and elegant as Waugh's, jumps off the page. The whole episode is angled so that Miss Vavasour and Jumbo emerge as figures of common sense, Mr Crouchback as unworldly and unselfish, and the Cuthberts as avaricious 'poor types' unable to recognize nobility of spirit. It may be that this is what Waugh required for the purposes of his plot. None the less, it leaves a distinct feeling that the Cuthberts are in some way being patronized and Grigshawe cut down to size for reasons related to class relations.

Characters in *Officers and Gentlemen*

8.11 If Grigshawe, because of his origins, is not 'officer material', what of those from 'better' backgrounds? Let us now look at individual characters more closely, and at Guy, Claire and Trimmer in particular.

Guy Crouchback

8.12   All we learn from the opening pages is that Guy is a member of a London club and that he is 'not a good mixer' as he deliberately flouts a request from a self-important Air Marshal and so loses a potential ally. We soon learn, however, that he is a man with a sense of honour and purpose:

> So Guy set out on the second stage of his pilgrimage, which had begun at the tomb of Sir Roger. Now, as then, an act of *pietas* was required of him; a spirit was to be placated. Apthorpe's gear must be retrieved and delivered before Guy was free to follow his fortunes in the King's service.
>
> (p.21)

8.13   The first stage of his pilgrimage began in *Men at Arms* when he decided to seek the King's commission. In that first volume we also learnt that his family was 'until quite lately rich and numerous', landed Catholic gentry with a martyr from the period of Reformation persecution. Guy's credentials for calling himself a gentleman in terms of the English socio-economic class system seem impeccable. He does not even, so far as we are told, have to work for his living. Yet does his religious allegiance set him apart as someone not quite conforming?

ACTIVITY

How, when he has eventually secured a commission, does Guy understand his calling?

DISCUSSION

It is not until late in the novel that we learn, retrospectively, Guy's feelings about the war he is to be drawn into. When he is convalescing after the Crete episode, we learn that

> It was just such a sunny, breezy Mediterranean day two years before when he read of the Russo-German alliance, when a decade of shame seemed to be ending in light and reason, when the Enemy was plain in view, huge and hateful, all disguise cast off; the modern age in arms.
>
> (p.240)

This self-admittedly naive understanding of politics produces a quixotic wish to join in. Guy's feelings about his part in the war are more than a little romantic; out of touch with reality, his disillusion when it comes is all the greater. As I point out in Radio 4 *Home and Abroad*, it begins in Alexandria before the action in Crete when Guy decides to go to confession but wants to do so away from the army:

> He wished to make his Easter duties and preferred to do so in a city church, rather than in camp. Already, without deliberation, he had begun to dissociate himself from the army in matters of real concern.
>
> (p.122)

The fact that the priest he finds for his purpose turns out to be a spy for the Germans compounds the sense that no one is to be trusted. Ivor Claire's desertion and the cover-up arranged by Julia Stitch are the last straw:

> He had no old love for Ivor, no liking at all, for the man who had been his friend had proved to be an illusion. He had a sense, too, that all war consisted in causing trouble without much hope of advantage.
>
> (pp.238–9)

BLOCK 3
'ENGLISHNESS'

So, when the alliance between Russia and the allies is announced, Guy feels that his previous perception of 'the Enemy' was merely an hallucination which has

> dissolved, like the whales and turtles on the voyage from Crete, and he was back after less than two years' pilgrimage in a Holy Land of illusion in the old ambiguous world, where priests were spies and gallant friends proved traitors and his country was led blundering into dishonour.
>
> (p.240)

For Guy, then, patriotism and honour are linked: to him Englishness and 'honour' – 'fidelity', 'truth' – go together. Although he suffers a general disillusion, Guy's own conduct has been, we are told in the closing pages, 'wholly creditable'.

ACTIVITY

On page 85 I suggested that it was inappropriate to call Guy the novel's hero. Can you now see why?

DISCUSSION

The novel doesn't have a hero in the conventional sense, though it has its villain in the form of Ivor Claire. Nevertheless, Guy does stand for certain values which it is implied have heroic quality: his disinterested sense of honour, romantic code of loyalty, patriotism and unworldly chivalry, all presented as laudable, are not only *masculine* but also in the context of the novel related to class, social position and national identity. Does this bring us back to a nostalgic notion of Englishness? Is Geoffrey Moore (whose view of the novel you will come to at the end of this section) correct to see Waugh as indulging in sentimental nostalgia for the 'days of privilege and order'? I think perhaps he is, though Waugh does it unashamedly both in this novel and elsewhere.

Ivor Claire

8.14 Ivor Claire, whom Guy first meets on the Isle of Mugg, certainly comes from the right socio-economic class to be a conventional officer: he is a 'young show-jumper of repute' and a member of Bellamy's (Guy's London club), and he moves in circles of influence and power which eventually rescue him from serious trouble. But is he a 'gentleman' or a man of honour? Guy thinks that he is and at the end of the Interlude, while on the way to Alexandria, thinks of him as 'the fine flower of them all. He was quintessential England, the man Hitler had not taken into account' (p.114).

8.15 These phrases are an interesting example of the way that Waugh manages to create, by careful preparation, two points of view simultaneously, for the words are presumably those going through Guy's mind yet any careful reader will know by now how deeply ironic they are, for Ivor Claire is the exact opposite of a 'fine flower'.

ACTIVITY

What signs can you find in the text that Claire is a 'bad lot'?

DISCUSSION

To make an entry wiping 'his dog's face with a silk handkerchief' and drinking Kümmel in a military establishment is not a good start. Then other clues are dropped as the narrative unfolds: his only interest in the welfare of Angus (who has had an accident) is in the effect of the morphia (p.50). On the night exercise (Book One, Section 9) we are told Ivor is lazy, only then to be presented with his ingenious if cheating way of getting home before anyone else. Strangely, this brings Ivor and Guy together, partly because the latter thinks he discerns 'with this most dissimilar man, a common aloofness, differently manifested ... thus with numberless reservations they became friends...' (p.87).

But to the alert reader further clues follow: it is not a good sign that Claire admits to knowing 'nothing of wine' and 'nothing of art' (p.108). Then, after his accident in Egypt, Claire 'installed himself in a private nursing-home' and, when visited by Guy, shows no interest in the war and seems concerned only about going to the races in Cairo. All this is by way of preparation for the final conversation Guy and Claire have about the meaning of honour, where it must be clear to every reader (though not to Guy) that Claire is justifying to himself his planned desertion:

> 'And in the next war, when we are completely democratic, I expect it will be quite honourable for officers to leave their men behind. It'll be laid down in King's Regulations as their duty – to keep a *cadre* going to train new men to take the place of prisoners.'
>
> (p.221)

He leaves Guy with the words 'the path of honour lies up the hill', which really means simply saving his own skin, or 'being fly', as he puts it. So although Guy thinks they have something in common, in reality they are opposites. Although Claire has the manners and background of a 'gentleman', he has not the honour which, in Guy's eyes, goes with it, and by his desertion could not in the army's terms consider himself still an officer. Nevertheless, by Julia Stitch's scheming, he gets away with it and nothing will be said, from which the moral seems to be 'don't get caught'.

Trimmer

8.16 Trimmer is a character Waugh has some fun with. His name comes from his background as a hairdresser on the ocean liner *Aquitania* where, under the name 'Gustave', he used to do Virginia's hair. He has been introduced in *Men at Arms* which is why Guy recognizes him on Mugg. Known alternately as Trimmer and McTavish, his real name remains a mystery, though both are used for the purposes of the plot. Unlike Guy, Trimmer did not get on with the Halberdiers and dismisses their pomp and ceremony as 'all that rot' (p.53). We're never told of his background but his familiarity with waiters and barmen during his weekend in Glasgow suggests it is from a lower socio-economic group than Guy's:

> The two men looked at one another, fraud to fraud. They had both knocked about a little. Neither was taken in by the other. For a moment Trimmer was tempted to say: 'Come off it. Where did you get that French accent? The Mile End Road or the Gorbals?
>
> The waiter was tempted to say: 'This isn't your sort of place, chum. Hop it.'
>
> (p.73)

8.17 He wouldn't seem to qualify as a 'gentleman' in terms of social groupings and his first act is to cheat the trust system of paying for drinks by signing someone else's name, though only of 'chaps I know would give me a drink if they were in'. But Trimmer plays a relatively small part in the novel's concern with the officer/gentleman issue: as he gets progressively drawn into the 'Popgun' episode and its consequences, he becomes more a figure for comedy. Where he is important is in a discussion of the theme of class, a subject near the heart of any discussion of Englishness, which I have already touched on and shall look at in more detail below.

Class and the 'people's war'

8.18 In discussing the scenes in the Marine Hotel earlier, I suggested that they were angled to show characters in good and bad lights in a manner related to their 'social class', and that this illustrated the English obsession with this issue. It is again brought to the fore in an unavoidable way in the relationship that develops between Virginia and Trimmer. Trimmer, whom we know to be a man on the make, goes to Glasgow for a weekend's fun, looking for a woman 'with all the panache of a mongrel among the dustbins'. (Waugh's use of canine imagery both here and with Hound is understandable given his dislike of dogs, though it makes the introduction of Mr Crouchback's dog Felix rather unconvincing.) What he finds in the hotel bar, sitting in her slightly ageing *grand couturier* clothes, is Virginia, who has '"class written all over her" as Trimmer inwardly expressed it'. ('Class' here means not 'social distinction' but 'style'.) The fencing that then goes on between them is entirely based on shifting class relationships: Trimmer, or 'Gustave', reminds her of the old days on board ship, but when he gets too personal – 'Boy friend?' – is immediately kept in check: 'You always were too damned fresh.'

8.19 When Virginia admits she is now hard up financially,

> Trimmer was both shocked and slightly exhilarated by this news.
>
> The barrier between hairdresser and first-class passenger was down. It was important to start the new relationship on the proper level – a low one.
> (p.76)

He attempts to do this by using her first name, but his self-consciousness encourages her to tease him, which leads him to tell her stories of his 'fun' with people 'of your set'. Their different backgrounds are neatly signalled by his failure to understand her advice to look first at prices on the menu, which causes Virginia to comment: 'Never mind. I expect there are all sort of things we don't "get" about one another' (p.77).

8.20 None the less, Virginia, who lives for the moment, decides he will do for a weekend, though she could hardly be more indifferent when he leaves hurriedly. When they meet up again in No.6 Transit Camp in London, the barriers are firmly in place in front of Kerstie:

> Virginia, as near as is humanly possible, was incapable of shame, but she had a firm residual sense of the appropriate. Alone, far away, curtained in fog – certain things had been natural in Glasgow in November which had no existence in London, in spring, amongst Kerstie and Brenda and Zita.
> (p.135)

8.21 Appropriately, it is Trimmer, the 'bare-kneed major with a cockney accent', who is to become the hero in Ian Kilbannock's publicity exercise, 'Popgun'. Earlier in the novel, Kilbannock has turned up at Mugg and, when slightly drunk, expatiated to Guy about the kind of war they are fighting.

There will be stories in the papers but not about Guy and his kind because they are

> '...Upper Class. Hopelessly upper class. You're the 'Fine Flower of the Nation'. You can't deny it and *it won't do*'.
>
> In the various stages of inebriation, facetiously itemized for centuries, the category, 'prophetically drunk', deserves a place.
>
> 'This is a People's War,' said Ian prophetically, 'and the People won't have poetry and they won't have flowers. Flowers stink. The upper classes are on the secret list. We want heroes of the people, to or for the people, by, with and from the people.'
>
> (p.101)

8.22 Given the contempt generously poured on Kilbannock throughout the novel culminating in the farce of 'Popgun', it is fairly safe to assume that, however seriously *he* takes this sentiment in his cups, Waugh's intention was to pour scorn on it. It is certainly noticeable that the only two non-upper-class characters to receive significant attention, Trimmer and Ludovic, are a joker and an eccentric respectively, and there is more than a hint of contempt for 'ordinary people'.

8.23 Yet the notion of a 'People's War' is surely not to be so lightly dismissed? Whatever Waugh's personal feelings about the idea, it was certainly one that existed at the time. Angus Calder has, as a social historian, written on the subject (1969, *The People's War: Britain 1939–45*), and other modern historians regard it as a valid notion. Many who knew Waugh have commented on his tendency to see the world as he wished to and, given his lack of time for those socially 'inferior' to himself, this novel may well illustrate that habit. In his defence, it could be argued that *artistically* he set deliberate limits to his range and that the title of the novel gives notice of this.

Gender in *Officers and Gentlemen*

8.24 The same arguments could be applied to the question of gender: is this a male version of history? There are in fact only eight female characters in the novel and only two of those play an active part in the plot. But Waugh chose to write about intensely male events. No doubt there are novels to be written about the invaluable work women did in the armed forces but such a subject was not within Waugh's scope and knowledge. More interesting to discuss in terms of gender is how maleness functions in the novel. We have already seen one instance of male bonding in the relationship of Guy and Tommy. Having loved and married the same woman, they are 'blood brothers' and their friendship is sealed 'on a plane rarer and loftier than normal human intercourse'. Another example of this occurs when Jumbo Trotter visits Mr Crouchback at the Marine Hotel and, having dined together, they find interests in common to discuss 'not competitively but in placid accord' (p.36). A little later, Bertie and Eddie get companionably drunk together in Cape Town. Maleness is seen favourably and positively in *Officers and Gentlemen*. When Miss Vavasour wants to pay Mr Crouchback a compliment, it is in these terms:

> Miss Vavasour had turned about and now was making for Mr Crouchback's sitting-room. He opened the door and stood back to admit her. A strong smell of dog met their nostrils.
>
> 'Such a nice manly smell,' said Miss Vavasour.
>
> (p.23)

8 EVELYN WAUGH: 'OFFICERS AND GENTLEMEN'

It seems also to be bound up with the notion of honour for, on the day Guy and Ivor have their discussion about whether or not it is something that can change, we are told that Guy

> had no clear apprehension that this was a fatal morning, that he was that day to resign an immeasurable piece of his manhood.
>
> (p.221)

Since we are told that Guy's subsequent adventure on the boat was 'wholly creditable' this can only mean that the defeat and surrender by the Allies was in itself discreditable and 'un-manning'.

ACTIVITY

Is there any significance, then, in the fact that it is Mrs Stitch who pulls the strings to get Ivor Claire out of trouble? Is this female subterfuge?

DISCUSSION

It is undeniably subterfuge, and of a cunningly clever kind, but I don't think Waugh relates it to gender, for Tommy Blackhouse shares Mrs Stitch's point of view:

> Tommy had his constant guide in the precept: never cause trouble except for positive preponderant advantage. In the field, if Ivor or anyone else were endangering a position, Tommy would have had no compunction in shooting him out of hand. This was another matter. Nothing was in danger save one man's reputation.
>
> (p.238)

ACTIVITY

The scene in which Ivor's escape is engineered deserves close attention. What technique does Waugh employ to convey to the reader that the remarkable Julia Stitch is at work on her mission, and does the narrative appear to endorse her scheming?

DISCUSSION

It is all done through dialogue, by implication and understatement. Nowhere does the narrative actually state that Mrs Stitch has got Claire 'off the hook'. The reader has to infer this from clues dotted in the dialogue: when Ritchie-Hook's name is mentioned, 'Mrs Stitch was suddenly alert' (p.241). When she then learns that he has a taste for vengeance, and that technically he has been Claire's superior, she suddenly becomes thoughtful:

> 'I see, I see,' said Mrs Stitch. 'And he's really been in command of Tommy's force all the time?'
>
> 'On paper.'
>
> 'And he's due when?'
>
> 'Before the end of the week, I gather.'
>
> 'I see. Well now, I must go and help Algie.'
>
> (pp.241–2)

In the following scene, Guy finds that he has been mysteriously posted back to England by the slowest route possible. Attempting to fulfil his obligation to the dead Catholic soldier, he hands an envelope with the identity disc to Mrs Stitch which she, assuming it to be a report of the withdrawal from Crete, immediately destroys:

> As he drove away she waved the envelope; then turned indoors and dropped it into a waste-paper basket. Her eyes were one immense sea, full of flying galleys.
>
> (p.244)

The metaphor Waugh uses to describe her eyes is mysterious and powerful, suggesting a huge blankness in which activity is paradoxically rife – an apt description of her own 'innocent' machinations which are not directly signalled in the narrative. 'Flying galleys' is also a reference to Cleopatra's ships deserting Antony at the Battle of Actium, for Mrs Stitch (like Virginia) is in her own way a disruptive, anti-heroic figure. 'Honour' is, according to Waugh, a male attribute and it is not without significance that Ivor Claire is effeminate in manner.

Moral issues in *Officers and Gentlemen*

ACTIVITY

'Simple rules of conduct' is the phrase used to describe the basis of Julia Stitch's actions – 'An old friend was in trouble. Rally round'. Yet we are told that Guy, the principal character and 'consciousness', 'lacked these simple rules'. Is this to say that they are implicitly criticized in the narrative?

DISCUSSION

I rather think they are, because there is no 'justice' in Claire's managing to get away with desertion while others die or languish in prison.

ACTIVITY

If this is so, what *is* offered in the text as a touchstone by which moral issues are decided?

DISCUSSION

In addition to (and linked with) the 'values' of an 'heroic quality' it has, surely, to be Guy's Roman Catholicism. This is the frame within which all three *Sword of Honour* novels are set, and in *Officers and Gentlemen* we see it most manifest, perhaps, in old Mr Crouchback, who teaches at 'Our Lady of Victory's Preparatory School'. In the course of a Latin lesson he is easily distracted into giving yet again an account of his martyred ancestor, Blessed Gervase.

ACTIVITY

What are we to think of Mr Crouchback and his function in the novel?

BLOCK 3
'ENGLISHNESS'

DISCUSSION

For me, there is a problem with Mr Crouchback. He is clearly meant to be a saintly, unworldly man, generous in his actions and conduct. (Waugh described him in a letter as 'admirable'.) Waugh works hard at this: he is described as a 'gentle, bewildered old man' (p.28) who is hardly in this world: a mere reference to *the wireless* almost causes contempt to well up within him. Mrs Tickeridge calls him a 'heavenly old man'; he is adored by his dog Felix and puzzled by his grandson's apparently self-centred letter from prison-camp listing all the material things he needs. (In *Unconditional Surrender*, the final novel in the trilogy, he becomes more explicitly a guide on moral issues with his often repeated dictum 'Quantitative judgements don't apply'. Yet, somehow it is difficult to believe in him. Even worse, his 'goodness' has a cloying, unconvincing quality – is he not a shade *too* self-sacrificing? Is he really this at all, when it comes down to it? And his manner of dealing with the Cuthberts who manage the Marine Hotel where he lives seems positively patronizing, though Waugh obviously intended it to be an example of *noblesse oblige*.

His son Guy, with his diffidence, his sense of failure and concern for justice, is a more convincing figure. Making his confession outside the army camp, we learn that to him these religious duties are one of the 'matters of real concern'. The Catholic liturgical year runs like a thread through the novel. Look at these examples:

> Guy was momentarily reminded of Holy Saturday at Downside; early gusty March mornings of boyhood; the doors wide open in the unfinished butt of the Abbey; half the school coughing; fluttering linen; the glowing brazier and the priest with his hyssop, paradoxically blessing fire with water.
> (p.9)

> It was All Souls' Day. Guy walked to church to pray for his brothers' souls – for Ivor especially; Gervase seemed so far off that year, in Paradise perhaps, in the company of other good soldiers.
> (p.41)

> On Holy Saturday 1941...
> (p.115)

> Outside, in the cathedral, whose tower could be seen from the War Office windows; far beyond in the lands of enemy and ally, the Easter fire was freshly burning.
> (p.116)

> Sprat returned to his office. All over the world, unheard by Sprat, the *Exultet* had been sung that morning.
> (p.117)

> When the first bells of Easter rang throughout Christendom...
> (p.118)

ACTIVITY

What is the effect of these references?

DISCUSSION

Waugh is properly putting Holy Week and the fire used at the Vigil Service at the heart of the liturgy to which he makes continual reference, as these examples illustrate. The *Exultet* is a joyful prayer of exhortation sung by the Cantor:

> *Exultet jam Angelica turba caelorum: exultent divina mysteria: et pro tanti Regis victoria, tuba insonet salutaris.*
>
> Rejoice, heavenly powers! Sing, choirs of angels! Exult, all creation around God's throne! Jesus Christ, our King, is risen! Sound the trumpet of salvation!

The fire indicates the new light of Christ and the victory over the powers of darkness: the Paschal candle is lit from the fire kindled in the brazier. The water in the font is then blessed with the newly lit candle and will be used throughout the following liturgical year for the baptism of new Christians into the life, death and resurrection of Jesus.

In 1941, the Vigil would have been on Saturday morning as Waugh describes it in the novel, though today it is usually late on Saturday evening to bring it as close as possible to the Resurrection on the third day. The cathedral Waugh refers to is Westminster Cathedral and the Cathedral Chronicle for that year states indeed that on 'Holy Saturday, April 12th, there was at 9.00 a.m. the Blessing of the Fire, Paschal Candle and Baptismal Font, followed at 11.00 a.m. by Pontifical High Mass'. All the events in the novel are set within a temporal framework extending far beyond the present: Guy and Mr Goodall pray on All Souls' Day for the dead to become 'ransomed', that is, received into Heaven; when convalescing, Guy is described as 'one immortal soul', and his concern for his fellow Christian, the dead soldier, has a religious dimension to it. Taking the red identity disc is a way of carrying out one of the traditional seven corporal works of mercy (p.206). In the end, it is not really temporal at all but a spiritual and typological act.

ACTIVITY

Is this religious context in any way exclusive? What effect does it have on the way the book is read?

DISCUSSION

My own view is that the essential and central Catholic element in the novel should not prove a barrier to readers of other faiths (or none) because, although it forms the book's moral pivot, it is not made the principal subject. (Waugh's Catholicism is the subject of Radio 4 *Home and Abroad*.) The narrative assumes it as a norm rather than attempting to evangelize, and Guy's practices are seen, if anything, as rather odd. Telling Tommy Blackhouse of his confession in Alexandria to the priest he suspects of being a spy, Guy adds by way of explanation: 'It's one of the things we have to do now and then' (p.140).

Another way of putting it might be that it is 'un-English': Catholics in England are sometimes called 'left-footers' because they are supposedly out-of-step with everyone else. Waugh's own position on this would have been that his church was the same church as that which had existed in pre-Reformation times in England. That is the point of the emphasis on the martyr Blessed Gervase, the priest who dies for the Faith. It is worth remembering, too, that Waugh not only wrote a life of Edmund Campion, the Jesuit martyr later beatified as one of the English martyrs, in 1970, but also had a spirited argument in the columns of the *New Statesman and Nation* with the historian Hugh Trevor-Roper over the meaning of the term 'recusancy', at the end of which he pointed out that: 'Mr Roper's family apostatised [renunciation of religious allegiance] more recently than mine' (in Amory, 1982, p.646, letter dated 11 January 1954).

Which was the true church for an Englishman to belong to? This was the very debate, you will recall, that Waugh had with John Betjeman.

Yet if many of the assumptions on which the narrative rests are not shared by the reader, or even objected to, do they then become a difficulty? The majority of Waugh's English readers are not, after all, Catholics, so what other qualities does the novel have to continue to attract readers?

Humour in *Officers and Gentlemen*

ACTIVITY

Did you find *Officers and Gentlemen* amusing? If you did, how would you describe the humour?

DISCUSSION

I find Waugh a wonderfully comic novelist (somewhat in the vein of Wodehouse, a writer whose gifts he revered), creating humour of various kinds. Perhaps uppermost in this volume is satire, usually the mark of a writer with a serious purpose, and Waugh's targets are none other than the army itself and, as we have seen, its 'officers and gentlemen'. Although he writes of regimental life with apparent affection, the army itself with its rules, confusions and frustrations is seen in a progressively less favourable light, more so as Guy's disillusion deepens. Let me take just three instances of this – Major Hound, 'Operation Popgun' and Colonel Grace-Groundling-Marchpole (as preposterous a name as could be devised).

The acquaintance used for the basis of the character Major Hound nearly took Waugh to the law courts in a libel action, though it is difficult to conceive of anyone willing to admit to the likeness. In the novel, Hound is seen as the worst product of any Army Staff College – he believes there should be an answer for every situation 'in the book' and is the master of the 'finest Staff College language'. We are told that he 'had chosen a military career because he was not clever enough to pass into the civil service' (p.119). His ineptitude as a soldier, his cowardice and bullying are ruthlessly exposed, beginning with his first fall from grace over bargaining for food with the men:

> The deal was done. Fido took his price of shame in his hand, the little lump of the flaky, fatty meat and his single biscuit. He did not look at Guy, but went away out of sight to eat. It took a bare minute. Then he returned to the centre of his group and sat silent with his map and his lost soul.
> (p.177)

The canine aspect to his name is then developed at length – at too great a length some critics have thought. His nickname is 'Fido'; he 'snuffles' and 'paws' Guy at night, has 'doggy perceptions' (p.202) just before his second 'fall', again over food. His fate finally at the hands of Ludovic remains somewhat obscure, but by this time Waugh's main point has been made. Hound represents a particularly rigid, unlikeable kind of army officer at whose expense he has considerable fun while making the serious point that he is also a completely ineffectual soldier, a liability in action rather than an asset.

'Popgun' and Ian Kilbannock's related activities mix satire with another kind of humour – farce. The satire is at the expense of both the army and the press. 'Popgun' is an entirely pointless expedition, mounted solely to save a Commando unit from extinction by superior officers engaged in army in-fighting. At a meeting which takes place on Holy Saturday,

> All over the world, unheard by Sprat, the *Exultet* had been sung that morning. It found no echo in Sprat's hollow heart. He called his planners to him and his liaison officer.
>
> 'They're out to do us down,' he reported succinctly. He need not name the enemy. No one thought he meant the Germans.
>
> (p.117)

(Notice, in passing, how Waugh deliberately sets human cynicism against the hope in the Resurrection.) Then follows an account of 'Popgun' where Waugh turns to writing that verges on pure farce: Ian, Trimmer and his men end up on mainland France instead of their intended island and, as Ian gets steadily drunk on whisky, as a result of which he begins his Noel Coward imitations, he almost gets run over by a train. By luck and telling lies, the members of the expedition manage to turn a drunken farce (reminiscent of *The Tempest*) into an heroic escapade that the press can work up for public consumption. At this point, Waugh brings in the *Daily Beast* (an old 'character' from his earlier novel *Scoop*, as is Julia Stitch from *A Handful of Dust*) which, with other papers, writes Trimmer/McTavish up as a working-class hero. In this way, the class issue comes up again: old Mr Crouchback, who from a photograph patronizingly thinks McTavish 'looks what he is – a hairdresser's assistant' (p.152), sees this as a great success of the British social system:

> 'That's what's so heartening. That's where we've got the Germans beaten ... We've got no junker class in this country, thank God. When the country needs them, the right men come to the fore. There was this young fellow curling women's hair on a liner ... Then war comes along. He downs his scissors and without any fuss carries out one of the most daring exploits in military history. It couldn't happen in any other country, Mrs Tickeridge.'
>
> (pp.151–2)

On the other hand, the *Daily Beast* and its proprietor Lord Copper seize on this opportunity in the class struggle, since Copper is said always to have 'had it in for the regular army – old school tie, and that sort of rot'. The *Daily Beast* is then described contemptuously by one army officer as 'making McTavish an example. Saying the army is losing its best potential leaders through snobbery.' Sprat, who was behind the whole operation, is told to find employment for McTavish/Trimmer which 'will satisfy those Labour fellows in the House of Commons that we know how to use good men when we find them' (p.155). (Note the ridiculing again of left-wing politics, though to be fair to Waugh few, if any, journalists or politicians in his fiction emerge unscathed.) The whole episode is comic writing of the highest order, switching from action to reaction through narrative and dialogue of the most pointed economical kind.

The sheer quality of Waugh's prose is also to be seen in the last of my three examples of the comic side of the novel – the activities of Colonel Grace-Groundling-Marchpole. Marchpole and his 'most secret department' are a running joke through *Sword of Honour*. Their activity (in the end entirely pointless) is to collect random and muddled information which in some God-like way Marchpole will use to redeem the world:

> Premature examination of his files might ruin his private, undefined Plan. Somewhere in the ultimate curlicues of his mind, there was a Plan. Given time, given enough confidential material, he would succeed in knitting the

entire quarrelsome world into a single net of conspiracy in which there were no antagonists, merely millions of men working, unknown to one another, for the same end; and there would be no more war.

(pp.78–9)

The first item he adds to Guy's file is a copy of the Nazi propaganda planted on Guy by the Laird of Mugg's mad niece. This was blown from Guy's hand by the wind on Mugg. Then, after the spy–priest episode in Alexandria, Hound's official report finds its way to his office:

And this letter, together with the original report, was photographed and multiplied and distributed and deposited in countless tin boxes. In time a copy reached Colonel Grace-Groundling-Marchpole in London.

'Do we file this under "Crouchback"?'

'Yes, and under "Box-Bender" too, and "Mugg". It all ties in,' he said gently, sweetly rejoicing at the underlying harmony of a world in which duller minds discerned mere chaos.

(p.141)

ACTIVITY

Marchpole is one of Waugh's more serious jokes. Can you see any significance in his name?

DISCUSSION

I don't think it is over-imaginative to see that 'Grace' figures in it, for Marchpole sees himself as part of a 'plan', though hardly that of Divine Providence which is what Waugh has in mind. There is a double irony in that final paragraph: he is, of course, deceiving himself – his unrelated, confused facts *are* 'mere chaos'. ('Chaos', remember, is what the universe is said to have been created from.) Yet, implies the narrative, there *is* an 'underlying harmony' and a providential care. The delicacy and economy with which Waugh conveys this is proof of writing that compels admiration and respect.

An 'underlying harmony' could be a way of describing plot: I want to conclude this discussion of *Officers and Gentlemen* by looking at another of Waugh's novelistic skills and going back to a question I raised at the beginning, the question of plot.

ACTIVITY

Think about the plot for a few moments. What was the point of the summary I asked you to make of Book One, 'Happy Warriors'?

DISCUSSION

I suggested that you jotted down a sentence or two about each section because my own experience of having read the novel many times is that it is not easy to remember the sequence of events. That this is so reveals several things about Waugh's narrative: it is complex and fast-moving. This calls for plotting of a high order. In fact, all the bits (or almost all of them) do 'fit' very neatly. The relationship of Trimmer and Virginia is a good example. The two meet up again in Glasgow (a good example of Genette's 'analepsis') for a short-lived affair. Then they come together again at a London transit camp

8 EVELYN WAUGH: 'OFFICERS AND GENTLEMEN'

where Virginia is working in Kerstie's canteen. During the course of the 'Popgun' episode, Trimmer conceives a real passion for Virginia, and the meeting with the American journalists becomes an occasion centred solely on her instead of the Anglo-American relations as Ian had intended. To see the full extent of the plotting skill, you really need to follow the narrative thread through all three volumes of *Sword of Honour*; Trimmer and a forlorn Virginia are left touring the north of England on a morale boosting exercise in the final pages of *Officers and Gentlemen*, but there is more to come in the final volume. Nevertheless, there is a sufficient number of varied episodes in this middle volume neatly tailored into a continuous sequence to illustrate my point about the plot.

When I said 'almost all' of the pieces fit together, I had in mind one incident which does not seem to have been satisfactorily resolved – the fate of Major Hound. It is clear from the synopsis of the two preceding volumes that appears at the beginning of *Unconditional Surrender* that we are supposed to have assumed Ludovic 'perpetrated or connived at his [Hound's] murder'. But if you look again at the end of Book Two, Section 5, you will see that this is far from clear: the colony of bats coming to life 'for no human reason' does not necessarily signal a murder, though one can see that it *might* in the light of Waugh's later statement, and the hint on page 184 that Ludovic would have killed the German motor-cyclist.

Another loose end is Guy's position at the end of *Officers and Gentlemen*: disillusioned after the withdrawal from Crete, yet keeping 'mum' about Claire, he returns to his regiment where, it is implied, he finds a certain peace of mind. Whether or not Waugh had a subsequent volume in mind at the time of writing, one feels that Guy's position is somewhat unresolved, though not to the point of making the novel seem unfinished.

8.25 I want to conclude by presenting you with some reactions to this novel, both critical and appreciative. You will find this useful to your study of the material in the next section on interpretation. As you will discover, Stanley Fish, an American critic, calls a group of people with a common understanding an 'interpretive community'. Is Christopher Sykes, a fellow Catholic and friend of Waugh's, part of 'an interpretive community'? Is Moore outside this, or part of another, different community?

> The story gets off to a rousing start with an air-raid and a typical Evelyn challenge to the demands of good taste: 'The sky over London was glorious, ochre and madder, as though a dozen tropic suns were simultaneously setting round the horizon...', soon to be followed by a description of a burning club, specially written, I think, for Henry Yorke, who served in the Fire Service throughout the war. 'On the pavement opposite Turtle's [club] a group of progressive novelists in firemen's uniform were squirting a little jet of water into the morning room.'
>
> From the beginning vividly drawn characters abound, but the most interesting do not come on the scene until half way through the first part. (The book is divided into two parts, 'Happy Warriors' and 'In the Picture', separated by an admirable 'Interlude' set in Cape Town and concluding with an 'Epilogue'.) The first character to arrest the reader's attention so that he says: 'Oh! This is something new! Not the usual stuff at all', is a dandified fellow officer called Ivor Claire. He is the first person whom the hero, Guy Crouchback, meets on being transferred from the imagined Halberdiers to the genuine Commandos. He only appears in this part of the trilogy. He is the *beau idéal* of British society, clever, impeccably dressed, a first-rate horseman, a born officer, the sort of man whom Evelyn was said to worship, and whom he did sometimes recklessly admire. But Ivor Claire turns out to be a man of putrefied core, only 'fair without'. He

BLOCK 3 'ENGLISHNESS'

treacherously deserts his men in the hour of crisis rather than go with them into captivity. The dialogue in which he tells Guy Crouchback of his pusillanimous decision is among a few which can be claimed as the finest Evelyn wrote at any time.

This is to go forward to the later parts of *Officers and Gentlemen*. Early in the story there appears one of the most preposterous characters in the whole of Evelyn's invention: the former hairdresser 'Trimmer', disguised as Captain, and occasionally Major, McTavish. He is compounded of fraud, artfully indicated by the fact that we never learn his real name. On this odious creature of his imagination Evelyn heaped all his scorn for 'the Century of the Common Man', a congenial task. The funniest single episode in the book is Trimmer's raid in which he leads a small Commando party in an attack on enemy installations on the north coast of France. Everything imaginable goes wrong, notably Trimmer's nerve, and the fiasco is covered up by publicity handled by the journalist Lord Kilbannock. This farce is brilliantly backed up by another. When Trimmer becomes a national hero, he turns out to be a Frankenstein's monster as well, and the sufferings of the Frankenstein Kilbannock and his friends at the hands of the monster are exploited by Evelyn with all his merciless skill...

As mentioned already, the long descriptive passage, possibly the best of Evelyn's sustained passages, in which, in the course of an occasionally and always craftily broken narrative of nearly a hundred pages, he tells of the great reverse in Crete, Evelyn modelled the story closely on the diary he kept at the time. Fiction is firmly placed before a background of experienced reality, except in the last episode, where Guy Crouchback and Corporal-Major Ludovic go through the ordeal of a long journey in an open boat from Crete to the African coast. This was not a thing that had happened to Evelyn, but had happened to many; an ordeal of which Evelyn must have heard first-hand accounts.

A fine novel, not open to criticism of essentials or essential points, with merits far outweighing blemishes.

(Sykes, 1975, pp.557–61)

Guy's adventures are surely not intented to be merely picturesque; it cannot be for nothing that he has been made both Catholic and anciently upper-class – although, of course, Mr Waugh's heroes rarely escape one or other of these distinctions. Should we take Guy's response to the war as having been misguided? Will Ivor Claire turn out not to have been a coward after all?

There is, too, the matter of the snobbery. One cannot explain it away, as some have tried to do. Mr Waugh loves a lord and is unremiss about it. It is all bound up with his view of life, which seems to be sentimental nostalgia for the days of privilege and order ... Social snobbery can be mildly funny, but it now looms so large in Mr Waugh's novels and is so seldom relieved by humour that it gives his work the edge of bigotry. There is so much attention to scoring off non-gentlemanly characters that Mr Waugh reads at times like the Frances Parkinson Keyes of the intellectuals.

It is not merely that the picture presented lacks perspective and chiaroscuro, it is that it is lopsided as well. Mr Crouchback Senior, for example, is a dear old gentleman, but his every appearance is the excuse for another act of unrelieved and fulsome goodness, and his lower-class foils are made as black as he is white. The grasping and common hotel-keepers, who are outwitted by his determined innocence, are even made to say to one another: 'Somehow his mind seems to work different than yours or mine.'

(Moore, 1984, p.375)

Summary of Book One

Book One is entitled 'Happy Warriors' (Waugh's original title for the whole novel – *Officers and Gentlemen* came from his American publisher). 'Happy Warriors' refers to the formation of the soldiers who are to see action in Book Two.

8 EVELYN WAUGH: 'OFFICERS AND GENTLEMEN'

Section 1

The air raid (the 'progressive novelists' putting out fires is Waugh's joke at the expense of the novelist Henry Yorke who joined the ARP). Guy's Catholic background and aristocratic connections are introduced. Guy is looking for a posting, under a cloud after the incident in *Men at Arms*.

Section 2

Guy reports to his regiment and gossips about the past. He is granted leave and sets out to carry out Apthorpe's dying wish.

Section 3

A winter evening at a Roman Catholic preparatory school. Guy's father is introduced and more background on Guy's Catholic ancestry. Officer/gentleman issue raised (p.24).

Section 4

Through Churchill's intervention and the bureaucracy of the army, Guy is forgiven for the Dakar incident. Jumbo Trotter goes to call him back to HQ. An account of army procedures. Picture of life in a wartime hotel and more on the 'saintly' Mr Crouchback.

Section 5

All Souls' Day 1940. Guy collects Apthorpe's belongings, and visits Mr Goodall, an old Catholic friend whom he later sees in church praying for the dead. Guy, helped by Jumbo, reports to HOO HQ and is posted for Commando training to the Isle of Mugg.

Section 6

Guy reports to the Isle of Mugg; meets Ivor Claire and Tommy Blackhouse, his CO. Initial impressions of Claire. Guy meets up with 'Trimmer', who he knew when in the Halberdier regiment and who fiddles free drinks. By coincidence, Guy finds the man to whom Apthorpe has left his belongings.

Section 7

Guy and Tommy dine with Colonel Campbell and his mad niece. Mention of 'below stairs'. Tommy and Guy enjoy themselves. Ivor Claire's gambling success, Guy and Tommy's shifting relationship and the issue of rank. Guy is dispatched to find Jumbo Trotter.

Section 8

November 1940. Trimmer goes to Glasgow where, 'with all the panache of a mongrel among the dustbins', he finds Virginia. Virginia is introduced. Colonel Marchpole's file on Guy (begun in *Men at Arms*) now includes the mad niece's Nazi propaganda. Trimmer is found out by fellow officer and departs speedily. Back at Mugg, Jumbo Trotter is settling in. Trimmer applies to join the Commandos to escape detection. Tommy hints to Guy that Mugg is a preparation for a real exercise somewhere warmer – Crete (p.83).

Section 9

Guy, with no job except as assistant to Ritchie-Hook (whom he met in *Men at Arms*) is acting ADC to Tommy. During a night exercise Claire shows 'initiative'. Guy thinks they have something in common and becomes friends with him. Trimmer, now a Commando, cannot be found a job. He is eventually given to the 'Specialist' unit. Guy pays a return visit to the mad laird with an obsession for explosives. Trimmer has also been to see him in his new 'Specialist' role. Dr Glendening-Rees arrives and is given the 'Specialists' for his dietary experiments.

BLOCK 3
'ENGLISHNESS'

Section 10

Mrs Stitch's yacht *Cleopatra* appears at Mugg, having been commandeered for war work. Its appearance at Mugg takes Guy back to his Italian home and memories of seeing her there. Ritchie-Hook disembarks and takes command of 'Hookforce'. Ian Kilbannock (first met in Section 1) tells Guy that the Commandos are due for an operation, and, when drunk, expounds on the 'People's War'. Next morning, the troopship sails. The mad laird steals explosives and the mad doctor is brought back on a stretcher.

9 *Meaning and interpretation*

9.1   As we saw in the concluding pages of Section 8, a literary text like *Officers and Gentlemen* can provoke very different reactions in readers, each of whom presumably believes his or her own reading to be valid. Do we think some readings are 'right' and others 'wrong'? Do we believe there is one 'right' interpretation or could there be several? Are all interpretations equally valid? These are fundamental questions in the study of literature at degree level and that is why the issue is raised here in the final section of Block 3. It is another part of the critical–theoretical debate within the course as a whole which I referred to in Section 5 when discussing the presentation of consciousness in fiction.

9.2   In this section of the block we shall be looking at the ideas of two American critics on the subject of interpretation before testing them out on texts in this block in a discussion between Peter Faulkner and me (Radio 5 *Is There a Text in this Programme?*). Then, armed with this knowledge and experience, the course team hope that you will be in a stronger position to encounter other texts later in the course.

ACTIVITY

Is there any difference between 'interpretation' and 'meaning'? Can you see how they might be said to differ?

DISCUSSION

Establishing 'meaning', I suggest, is the *practical exposition* of a text. It means explaining a text, pointing out references, commenting on the form, eliciting a meaning, establishing *what happens*. 'Interpretation', on the other hand, is more to do with adopting a certain view of a text. Or, to put it another way, a text may have a *meaning* but can be *interpreted in different ways*. Let me give you an example. In reading the Eliot poems in Block 2, you might find you need notes to help you establish Eliot's meaning (for example, what are the allusions, and why does he make them?). But you would still need to decide what you thought *The Waste Land* was really about. Was it in part the product of an ailing civilization or, if not that, an expression of something in Eliot's personal life?

Of course, you might be thinking at this point that these are difficulties dreamed up by academics to perplex their listeners. Why make difficulties if it is clear that Eliot *was* referring to European civilization, or that Waugh wanted to write a novel about the Second World War? Unfortunately, it isn't that simple, for experience shows us that over the centuries people *do* understand texts differently. (Libraries of academic criticism are witness to this fact.) For example, in the nineteenth century Shakespeare tended to be read like a novelist (at a time when that was the dominant literary form). At the beginning of the twentieth century, he was regarded more as a poet. E.D. Hirsch Jr distinguishes between the 'meaning' of a text (which he sees as stable) and 'understanding', that is, what later generations of readers make of a text in successive historical/cultural situations.

It has to be said at this point that not all critics think the distinction between *meaning* and *interpretation* is valid. It *can* be argued that the meaning of a text resides *only* in the way it is interpreted, though this is taking 'meaning' in a broader sense than I have used it above. This, in fact, is the view taken by the first of our two American critics, Stanley Fish. You will quickly see that if he is right, one text is likely to have *many* different interpretations. Is, then, any agreement possible about what a text means, or are all texts doomed to the instability of numerous interpretations? Or is this instability something to welcome?

ACTIVITY

Let us now look at how Stanley Fish sees the business of interpreting the text. Please read the extract from 'Interpreting the *Variorum*', pages 55–62 in the Reader. What are Fish's main points in the opening paragraphs?

DISCUSSION

Quite early in his discussion Fish refers to the 'interpretive act' and it is clear that, for him, interpretation of a text is an active, living experience, not an exercise that can be performed along predictable 'grammatical' or 'statistical' lines (for example, counting the active verbs). He goes on to the notion of 'interpretive strategies', that is, the means by which each person has chosen to make sense of a piece of writing. He then examines the convention of alliteration as an example of this. Alliteration only works, he argues, because in both written and spoken language certain rules have been agreed about repetition, its effect and desirability. This leads him to the conclusion that 'the choice is never between objectivity and interpretation but between an interpretation that is unacknowledged as such and an interpretation that is at least aware of itself'.

In other words, *all* forms of conscious thought are, in effect, 'interpretations', and it is better to be aware of this than to assume that there *is* such a thing as an objective examination of a text which simply exists 'out there' as a thing to be dissected. Of course, in taking this stand Fish is asking a question about how we perceive the world about us. Perhaps he is right to be open about the problems his view of interpretation raises, the most obvious of which is the danger of sliding into a hopeless relativism where nothing is fixed and no conclusions at all can be reached, except that there *are* no conclusions to be reached.

ACTIVITY

There are those to whom this is an acceptable position, but Fish is not one of their number. How does he avoid this?

9 MEANING AND INTERPRETATION

BLOCK 3
'ENGLISHNESS'

DISCUSSION

He escapes a 'random succession of forms' and achieves a 'stability of interpretation among readers' by the ingenious notion of 'interpretive communities'. This idea is consistent with Fish's belief in reading as something active. The fact that he and another reader might agree on the meaning of Milton's poem *Lycidas* does not mean that the poem has an objective, fixed meaning 'out there'. Rather, it shows that Fish and his fellow reader are using the same strategies as they 'write' Milton's text in an interpretive act, and in doing so they form a 'community'. By 'write' Fish doesn't mean literally in the sense of pen and paper, but metaphorically. For Fish really does mean that the *reader* produces the text: this is a view common to much recent literary theory, some of which is known as 'reader-response' for fairly obvious reasons. (The idea can be found in an essay in the Reader by the French critic Roland Barthes entitled 'The death of the author'.) Inevitably, in Fish's way of reading, the emphasis has moved decisively towards the reader as *providing the meaning* rather than what is read *having a single stable meaning*. The logical consequences of this *could* be to make all texts one since they are all realized, or 'written', by the same mind(s): this is the point of reference to St Augustine, in whose thinking all things were, or could be, conducive to realizing the love of God for his creation.

ACTIVITY

So has Fish achieved a stability of reading through the communal act of reading?

DISCUSSION

Only up to a point, for as he admits 'communities ... being living organisms ... develop and change' and so their stability is only temporary. Their stability is also limited by the fact that the strategies employed by their members are not 'natural' but 'learned', and what is 'learned' can be changed and modified.

Fish ends by asking whether he has not reintroduced the idea of 'encoded' meanings, that is, meanings concealed behind a code known only to initiates. It seems that, up to a point, he has because it is a consequence of his belief that the author assumes certain 'marks' will have meanings for his readers. But what I think he is really trying to do is generate a sense that the relationship of reader to text is something alive and shifting. (This relationship can, after all, be seen to exist *physically* and is familiar as a fact of any reading experience.) In this attempt, Fish finds himself in some philosophical tight corners from which, in his final paragraph, he appears to be escaping by the simple expedient of saying, 'If you understand me, you understand me'. But this explanation is not sufficient for some of his readers, as we shall see in the next extract by Robert Scholes. You have already met some of the ideas of this critic in Section 6 of Block 2 when, in discussing poetic language, Graham Martin introduced the idea that the use of language in a fictional situation was different from situations where the originator was present and could confirm or deny meaning.

ACTIVITY

In this extract Scholes is also concerned with establishing meaning in and through language, and it is on this point that he takes issue with Fish. Please now read 'Who cares about the text', pages 63–7 in the Reader, and summarize Scholes's main objections to Fish's argument.

DISCUSSION

Scholes's main objection is that Fish takes up what he sees as an 'extreme' position on the question of texts, and he challenges the assertion that 'texts have no properties of their own, that they are always only what their readers make of them'. To illustrate his point, he takes the example of two possible translations of the Hebrew Bible, one of which is open to two possible meanings, the other not. From this, he moves on to the question of the language in which the text is 'encoded', insisting that 'text is bound to its language'; it exists as a text only in and through its language. At the same time, it is not bound to any particular 'interpretive community'. (For example, *England Made Me* was created by Greene, using his native English, but it is not thereby confined to English or English-speaking readers – it can be translated into another language for other communities.) Language, he goes on to explain, has a number of *rules* but allows a lot of freedom of movement within them, just as a game of chess does.

Scholes then moves on to what Fish means by an 'interpretive community' and challenges the idea that meanings are *imposed* and constrained by the community of which the reader is part. He attacks what he sees as the vagueness of Fish's definition of an 'interpretive community', pointing out that it can mean various things at various times. (Do war veterans, for example, form a particular 'interpretive community' for *Officers and Gentlemen*? Do readers who share Waugh's Roman Catholicism form another? I shall come back to these questions later.) It is not simply the vagueness, as he sees it, of Fish's notion that Scholes objects to: he also resents the totalitarian notion of his assertion that a 'set of interpretive assumptions is always in force' because he wants to stress the individuality of the reader who, whether part of a particular community or not, will bring his/her 'different', even conflicting, assumptions to the text.

Pursuing his concentration on the language of a text, Scholes proceeds to define the relationship of both reader and writer to the linguistic code which gives meaning to the 'marks' of a printed text: the reader can only react to what the writer has previously chosen to place on the page. This, he argues, is how meaning is established, not by 'interpretive communities'. Scholes then turns to another feature of 'interpretive communities': 'principled debate', he says, is not possible or necessary within Fish's 'communities' because, by definition, its members have no disagreements. Logically, then, there must be as many 'communities' as there are interpretations. Are Fish's 'communities' the same, then, as critical schools – Freudian, feminist, Marxist? If not, what are they? And how can anything be established if debate is not possible?

The last two paragraphs in the extract in the Reader sum up Scholes's objections to Fish's ideas: they are dangerous because they contain an element of truth – consensus *is* reached by discussion, and discussion couched in a common language by people who could be said to form a community. But that is not to say that meaning is *only* established in this way. Nor should it deny that the text exists in one sense as a set of inked marks on the page (that is, print) representing an agreed linguistic code. This is really Scholes's main point; as he puts it in his final paragraph, in words that are perhaps intended to be a parody of the kind of 'sloganizing' he sees in Fish's work, 'Textual power is ultimately power to change the world'. Such power is dangerous, and for that very reason, to refuse to allow texts to possess any real stability, however temporary, is to play the sorcerer's apprentice with all its uncontrollable consequences.

9.3   Now let me return to those questions posed earlier about readers of *Officers and Gentlemen*. Is there a 'retired officer Catholic reader'? (The author certainly fell into the last category.) I think the answer to this has to be 'yes

BLOCK 3
'ENGLISHNESS'

... up to a point'. A reader who was a veteran of the Cretan campaign would, for example, scrutinize the Crete chapters of the novel much more carefully than one who had never been involved in it. A Catholic reader would know what form the 'Easter Fire' took. As such, in Fish's terms, each belongs (though in a non-exclusive way) to an 'interpretive community'. On the other hand, assuming that they are, in Scholes's terms, 'competent interpreters' (that is, experienced in encountering texts), neither would assume that their particular focus constituted the entire 'meaning of the novel', for their personal response is to only *part* of the text, a text that exists indubitably as 'marks on the paper'. I am sure that you will be able to find many more examples for yourself. Do *female* readers find Eliot and Waugh misogynistic, and do *male* readers even think about this aspect of their writing? Do the answers to these questions mean that there will forever be at least two huge communities throughout the world? Or is gender not that binding? I don't know the answer to these questions. I put them to you to consider and debate.

9.4 Lastly, please cast your mind back to Section 1 of this block. You will recall that we examined a number of 'texts' there, an extract from Virginia Woolf's *Three Guineas* being one of them. Was the way in which you came to your view of the block theme of 'Englishness' influenced by one or more 'interpretive communities' you might feel yourself to be part of, a community determined by race, gender, religion or position in society? Now that we have come to the end of Block 3, spend a while before going on to the tutor-marked assignment revising your thoughts about 'Englishness'. Has your initial view of it been modified by the literary texts you have worked through? Has your view of those texts been modified in turn by the ideas you have encountered in this last section?

10 References

ALLAIN, M.F. (1984) *The Other Man*, Penguin.

AMORY, M. (ed.) (1982) *The Letters of Evelyn Waugh*, Penguin.

ANDERSON, P. (1969) 'Components of the national culture', *New Left Review*, 50, pp.3–57.

AUDEN, W.H. (1932) *The Orators*, Faber.

AUDEN, W.H. (1936) *Look, Stranger!*, Faber.

BALDICK, C. (1983) *The Social Mission of English Criticism 1848–1932*, Clarendon Press.

BALDWIN, S. (1937) *On England*, Penguin (first published 1926).

BERGONZI, B. (1978) *Reading the Thirties*, Macmillan.

BETJEMAN, J. (1932) *Mount Zion*, John Murray.

BETJEMAN, J. (1937) *Continual Dew*, John Murray.

BETJEMAN, J. (1945) *New Bats in Old Belfries*, John Murray.

BETJEMAN, J. (1954) *A Few Late Chrysanthemums*, John Murray.

BETJEMAN, J. (1958) *Collected Poems*, John Murray.

BETJEMAN, J. (1960) *Summoned by Bells*, John Murray.

REFERENCES

BETJEMAN, J. (1966) *High and Low*, John Murray.

BETJEMAN, J. (1982) *Uncollected Poems*, John Murray.

BLUNDEN, E. (1943) *Cricket Country*, Collins.

BRIGGS, A. (1982) 'The English: custom and character' in BLAKE, R. (ed.) *The English World: history, character and people*, Thames and Hudson.

CALDER, A. (1969) *The People's War: Britain 1939–45*, Jonathan Cape.

CARDUS, N. (1934) *Good Days*, Hart-Davis.

COHN, D. (1978) *Transparent Minds: narrative modes for presenting consciousness in fiction*, Princeton University Press.

COLLS, R. and DODD, P. (eds) (1986) *Englishness: politics and culture 1880–1920*, Croom Helm.

DONALDSON, F. (1982) *P.G. Wodehouse: a biography*, Weidenfeld and Nicolson.

DOYLE, B. (1986) *English and Englishness*, Methuen.

EDWARDS, O. DUDLEY (1977) *P.G. Wodehouse: a critical and historical essay*, Martin Brian and O'Keeffe.

ELIOT, T.S. (1922) *The Waste Land*, Faber.

ELIOT, T.S. (1944) *Four Quartets*, Faber.

FORSTER, E.M. (1936) *Abinger Harvest*, Edward Arnold.

GREEN, B. (1983) *P.G. Wodehouse: a literary biography*, Oxford University Press.

GREENE, G. (1970a) *England Made Me*, Penguin (first published 1935, Heinemann).

GREENE, G. (1970b) *England Made Me*, Bodley Head (collected edition).

GREENE, G. (1980) *Ways of Escape*, Bodley Head.

HILL, G. (1968) *King Log* ('September Song'), Deutsch.

HORN, P. (1984) *Rural Life in England in the First World War*, Gill and Macmillan.

LESSING, D. (1968) *In Pursuit of the English*, Sphere.

LONGLEY, E. (1986) *Poetry in the Wars*, Bloodaxe.

LUCAS, J. (1986) *Modern English Poetry – from Hardy to Hughes*, Batsford.

MARCH, R. and TAMBIMUTTU (eds) (1948) *T.S. Eliot: symposium*, P.L. Editions Poetry.

MARSH, E. (ed.) (1912) *Georgian Anthology*, The Poetry Bookshop.

MENDELSON, E. (ed.) (1977) *The English Auden: poems, essays and dramatic writings 1927–1939*, Faber and Faber.

MENDELSON, E. (1981) *Early Auden*, Faber.

METHUEN, SIR A. (1921) *Anthology of Modern Verse*, Methuen.

MOORE, G. (1955) 'Review of *Officers and Gentlemen*', *New York Times Book Review*, 10 July 1955, reprinted in STANNARD, M. (1984) *Evelyn Waugh, The Critical Heritage*, Routledge and Kegan Paul.

MORRIS, J.H.C. (1981) *Thank You, Wodehouse*, Weidenfeld and Nicolson.

MORTON, H.V. (1927) *In Search of England*, Methuen.

MULHERN, F. (1979) *The Moment of 'Scrutiny'*, New Left Books.

NEWBOLT, H. (1921) *The Newbolt Report: the teaching of English in England*, HMSO.

ORWELL, S. and ANGUS, I. (eds) (1968) *The Collected Essays, Journalism and Letters of George Orwell, Volume III*, Secker and Warburg.

OWEN, W. (1931) *Poems*, Viking Press.

OWEN, W. (1967) *Collected Letters*, Oxford University Press.

SHERRY, N. (1989) *The Life of Graham Greene, Volume 1, 1904–1939*, Cape.

SMITH, S. (1986) *Edward Thomas*, Faber.

SPEARS, M.K. (1963) *The Poems of W.H. Auden: the disenchanted island*, Oxford University Press.

STEAD, C.K. (1967) *The New Poetic: Yeats to Eliot*, Penguin.

STEPHEN, L. (ed.) (1885–1900) *Dictionary of National Biography*, Oxford University Press.

SYKES, C. (1975) *Evelyn Waugh: a biography*, Collins.

THE OPEN UNIVERSITY (1986) DE354 *Beliefs and Ideologies*, Study Guide 2 'Politics and Ideology', The Open University.

THOMAS, E. (1906) *The Heart of England*, J.M. Dent.

USBORNE. R. (1976) *Wodehouse at Work to the End*, Barrie and Jenkins.

VOORHEES, R.J. (1966) *P. G. Wodehouse*, Twayne.

WARNER, V. (ed.) (1981) *Charlotte Mew: collected poems and prose*, Carcanet.

WAUGH, E. (1952) *Men at Arms*, Chapman and Hall.

WAUGH, E. (1961) *Unconditional Surrender*, Chapman and Hall.

WAUGH, E. (1964) *Officers and Gentlemen*, Penguin (first published 1955, Chapman and Hall).

WIDDOWSON, P. (ed.) (1982) *Re-Reading English*, Methuen.

WODEHOUSE, P.G. (1930) *Very Good, Jeeves!* Jenkins.

WODEHOUSE, P.G. (1961) *Performing Flea: a self-portrait in letters*, Penguin (first published 1953).

WOOLF, V. (1938) *Three Guineas*, The Hogarth Press.

The Jeeves canon – a note

Jeeves first features in one story in *The Man with Two Left Feet* (1917). By 1974, he had appeared in nineteen books by Wodehouse. Of the fifteen entirely devoted to his exploits, eleven were full-length novels – from *Thank You, Jeeves* (1934) to the suggestively titled *Aunts Aren't Gentlemen* (1974). Among these *The Code of the Woosters* (1938) and *The Mating Season* (1949) can be strongly recommended.

Acknowledgements

Grateful acknowledgement is made to the following for permission to reproduce material in this block:

de la Mare, W. (1915) 'All That's Past' from *Poems of Today: an anthology*, Sidgwick and Jackson (reproduced by kind permission of the Literary Trustees of Walter de la Mare and The Society of Authors as their representative); Auden, W.H. (1977) 'A Summer Night', 'A Bride in the 30s', 'Perhaps', 'The Malverns', 'Birthday Poem', 'Paysage Moralisé', 'XXIV' and 'Letter to Lord Byron, Part III' from *The English Auden: poems, essays and dramatic writings 1927–1939*, edited by Edward Mendelson, Faber and Faber; Auden, W.H. (1976) 'Miss Gee' from *Collected Poems*, Faber and Faber; Greene, G. (1935) *England Made Me* (extracts), Heinemann; Betjeman, J. (1982) 'An Ecumenical Invitation' and 'Christmas' from *Uncollected Poems*, John Murray.

Block 1   Introduction

Block 2   The Impact of Modernism

Block 3   'Englishness'

Block 4   Literature and Ideology

Block 5   End of Empire

Block 6   New Writings in English

Block 7   Language and Gender

Block 8   Literature and History

Cover illustration: Peter J. Manders, view of the bridge over the River Arrow at Eardisland, Herefordshire, 1972, scraper board drawing. Reproduced by permission of the artist.